JESUS CHRIST

IS COMING

AGAIN

[Behold I come quickly. Rev.22:12]

DR DAISY M LAKE

JESUS CHRIST

IS COMING AGAIN

Scripture quotations are taken from the King James
Version of the Bible unless otherwise stated.

Copyright © by Dr Daisy M Lake

ISBN 978-0-9565912-0-3

Published 2012 in the United Kingdom by:
EsteemWorld Publications in association with
Apostolic Publishing
22 Eastleigh Avenue
South Harrow
Middlesex UK
HA2 0UF

British Library Cataloguing In Publication Data
A Record of this Publication is available from the British
Library.

CONTENTS

5

DEDICATION

My greatest honour, respect, commitment and dedication, must first go to King Jesus, my precious Lord and Saviour, who has given me the motivation, by the power of his Holy Spirit, to write this book.

Secondly, I would like to dedicate this work to all my caring and loving children, my many grandchildren and great grandchildren. I thank the Lord for allowing me to be still with them and by the mercies of the Lord, I hope to be with them much longer, for the Lord's glory.

Thirdly, I add my dedication to all the wonderful ministers and saints of our various assemblies, at home and abroad, who stand with me in the ministry of the gospel.

I thank you all for loving and supporting me as I labour for the Lord.

God bless you all.

Dr Daisy Lake

ACKNOWLEDGEMENT

Firstly, I would like to acknowledge with all the thanks in the universe, the love, tender mercies and kindness of my precious Lord and Saviour, Jesus Christ, who has inspired me by the power of the blessed Holy Spirit to put pen to paper again to write this book. This is a book written by revelation, like all my other books. This book is a message to the Church of the Lord Jesus Christ in particular, and to the world in general. It was during my usual prayer time one morning that the Lord opened my spiritual eyes in a new way to the condition of spiritual and moral decay that prevails today worldwide; what is happening and what is to happen. It is a wake-up call to us all.

Secondly, I must acknowledge the support of my lovely daughter, Pastor Judy, for all her help in the office to allow me to find time to write. I must also thank and acknowledge my dear grandson, Jonathan, who does the covers for my books, and this book is no exception.

Thirdly, I acknowledge with many thanks the hard work of all our Ministers at home and abroad; all who have stood with me in the difficult times and in the good times. A big Thank You to all who have prayed for me and are praying for me as I strive to fulfil the will of the Lord for my life, which is ministering the gospel of our Lord Jesus Christ, so that men may repent and turn to him. The Lord's desire is that man may escape the damnation of hell.

Thank you all and may the Lord forever bless you.

INTRODUCTION

Mark 13:37   And what I say unto you, I say unto all, Watch.

I was recently praying and having my quiet time in the morning with my Lord. Suddenly, the burden of the state of the world was opened up to me in a new way. The Lord began to talk to my spirit man about the state of this very nation in which we live. The Lord showed me the lethargic state of the church: the decadence in the land in particular, and in the world in general. The Lord reminded me that he died to prevent people going to hell, which is a terrible place of torment, prepared for the devil and his angels. The Lord is very sad that multitudes are on the slippery slope down into the dark realms where satan and his demons abide; the place of complete evil.

When I remembered that many of my own grandchildren are not saved, I began to cry. I was brokenhearted. The Lord commanded me to preach the message at home and broad about His Coming and that I should warn the people to Watch. As soon as I had finished my prayers I got pen and paper and began to search the scriptures again to see what the bible says about the matter. The Lord worked with me as I checked scriptures. I began to do a summary of what I needed to preach. The Holy Spirit was at work in me and I just became so filled up, I wrote down many scriptures. As I wrote, several scriptures seemed to flow into my spirit. The Lord then told me of a church where I should go that very Sunday and minister this Word; the Lord spoke to me that the church was not at the place of holiness. I went and was called upon to minister. I did as the Lord commanded.

I told the church they were not living a life pleasing to the Lord. I found there was a lot to say. The following week I went to another church where I ministered the message the Lord gave me. There was so much to say and there was never going to be enough time to minister all the Lord was revealing to me. The Lord stood with me; the message was well received and they asked that I come again to complete the message.

I had told the Lord that I would not be writing any more books, but all of a sudden an overflow of joy came into my heart, to write down all that the Lord was revealing to me in a book.

As the Lord has led me, I have written about how man had sinned; lost the first dominion; how the Lord foreshadowed the coming of Christ to deliver man from sin and satan; how the prophets foretold the coming of Christ to save man; and how Jesus came and stood between man and the devil and hell by the power of his precious, shed blood.

I have tried to make my readers see how terrible hell is and how wonderful heaven is. If the reader will submit to the Lordship of Christ by accepting his free salvation he will enjoy the beauties and blessings of heaven, a place full of joy and peace. The devil is a rebel and deceiver and is doing all he can to drag man down to hell to the place where they will share with him total misery; a place where their worm dieth not and the fire is not quenched. *[Mark 9:44]*.

My hope is that our blessed Lord Jesus will minister to the hearts of the readers by his Holy Spirit and bring those who are not saved to a knowledge of the truth. I also trust that the church of the Lord Jesus Christ will see the urgency of the hour; awake and run with the gospel; put away sin; clean up her act and live for the Lord's glory before it is too late.

***Revelation 22:17** And the Spirit and the bride say, Come. And let him that heareth say, Come. And let him that is athirst come. And whosoever will, let him take the water of life freely.*

***Ecclesiastes 12:13-14** Let us hear the conclusion of the whole matter: Fear God and keep his commandments: for this is the whole duty of man. For God shall bring every work into judgment, with every secret thing, whether it be good, or whether it be evil.*

May the Lord forever bless you as you read this book, for the Lord's praise and glory and for your eternal benefit.

CHAPTER 1

THE FIRST COMING OF THE LORD REVEALED

Genesis 3:15 And I will put enmity between thee and the woman, and between thy seed and her seed; it shall bruise thy head, and thou shalt bruise his heel.

If Christ is to come again he must have come at least once before , and most of us know, even a little, about how and why he came. I will explain this below.

The account is detailed in the book of *Genesis, chapters 1-3*. I will quote a few verses only from these chapters. [Read *Genesis 1-3]*.

God Made Man
Genesis 1:26-29   26. And God said, let us make man in our image after our likeness: and let them have dominion over the fish of the sea , and over the fowl of the air, and over the cattle, and over all the earth, and over every creeping thing that creepeth upon the earth. 27. So God created man in his own image, in the image of God created he him; male and female created he them. 28. And God blessed them, and God said unto them, Be fruitful, and multiply, and replenish the earth, and subdue it; and have dominion over the fish of the sea, and over the fowl of the air, and over every living thing that moveth upon the earth.

God was creating; the bible says that God said, *"and it was so"*.

12

[Genesis 1:7 last clause]. The Lord God created every living thing : He created the firmament, the waters [the seas and rivers], the sun and moon, the grass and all the fruit trees. He created the birds of the air, the fish of the sea, the living creatures in the waters etc. God paired them all off, after their kind, blessed them and told them to be fruitful and multiply. God looked at all that he had created so far, and behold it was very good; God was pleased with his creation. As far as God was concerned, his creation would not be complete without man, so God said, Let us make man in our image, after our likeness... This amazes me because I think God made man after both his spiritual and physical likeness. I believe that is the reason Jesus took on the form of man to minister to man's needs. God made man to be his special friend and companion. He had a special love for man and I believe God was heart-broken when man sinned. I won't say anymore on this now; I will leave it until further on in the book. Like the animals and birds, God told man to be fruitful and multiply, but he also told man to replenish the earth, subdue it, and have dominion over all his other creation. Man should rule over God's other creation. Man was a prince with God. He was sharing rulership with his Maker. God gave man great authority, praise the Lord.

Some details as to how man was made by God:
Genesis 2:7-9, 17-18, 21-24 *7. And the Lord God formed man of the dust of the ground, and breathed into his nostrils the breath of life; and man became a living soul. 8. And the Lord God planted a garden eastward in Eden; and there he put the man whom he had formed. 9. And out of the ground made the Lord God to grow every tree that is pleasant to the sight, and good for food; the tree of life also in the midst of the garden, and the tree of the knowledge of good and evil. 17. But of the tree of the*

13

knowledge of good and evil thou shalt not eat of it: for in the day that thou eatest thereof thou shalt surely die. 21. And the Lord God caused a deep sleep to fall upon Adam, and he slept; and he took one of his ribs, and closed up the flesh thereof. 22. And the rib, which the Lord God had taken from man, made he a woman, and brought her unto the man. 23. And Adam said, This is now bone of my bones, and flesh of my flesh: she shall be called Woman, because she was taken out of the Man. 24. Therefore shall a man leave his father and his mother, and shall cleave unto his wife, and they shall be one flesh.

God formed man of the dust of the ground. This is surely a miracle. We see so many beautiful people every day, some are so proud and full of themselves, but what is man? Man's outer covering is dust. However God's Spirit is in man which gives life to the dust of the ground. We tend to forget that whenever God takes his Spirit out of us, we go right back to be just dust. What is there to be proud about? Man is completely dependent upon the Lord to stay alive.

After the Lord had formed the man and breathed into him the breath of life; the Lord looked upon this beautiful man, lovely and handsome and felt good about him. However, the Lord saw that all his other creation had a mate. The Lord realised that the man would be lonely and needed a companion. God did something so wonderful; he put the man to sleep and took a rib from his side and made a companion. Man was made to give pleasure to the Lord. God allowed the man to name the animals. After he had formed Adam's mate he brought her to the man and allowed him to name her. Adam, with the wisdom of God, called her Woman because she was taken out of the man. The woman is a part of the man so the man would not be

14

able to live without the woman; his wife. God is truly amazing!!

Man was made to live forever with his Maker having full fellowship with him, and in order for this to be so the Lord gave the couple strict orders as to what they should do and not do. They could eat of every tree of the garden except for the tree of the Knowledge of Good and of Evil. Since God had given so much authority and rulership to man, the Lord gave man the choice to be obedient to him, or otherwise. Man should be mature enough to make the right choice. God wanted man to serve him because he loves God and respects the Lord's supremacy. God did not want man to become a robot, just to be made to do as he is told without being able to say Yes or No. To use a well-used word: Man blew it. He made the wrong choice and the human race is still paying the price and will continue to do so until the end of the age. However, God had made provision from the foundation of the world to deliver man after he had sinned. The Lord knew man would go astray, but he allowed him to do so.

What are we to learn from this?
God has given us choice :

a] We should listen to the voice of God as he reminds us of his holy Word.

b] It is in our own interest to do what is right; we will save ourselves much suffering.

c] Disobedience brings the curse.
Man sinned, but the provision to deliver man was already made by God.

15

Genesis 3:1-10, 14-15 Now the serpent was more subtil than any beast of the field which the Lord God had made. And he said unto the woman, Yea, hath God said, Ye shall not eat of every tree of the garden? 2. And the woman said unto the serpent, We may eat of the fruit of the trees of the garden: 3. But of the fruit of the tree which is in the midst of the garden, God hath said, Ye shall not eat of it, neither shall ye touch it, lest ye die. 4. And the serpent said unto the woman, Ye shall not surely die. 5. For God doth know that in the day ye eat thereof, then your eyes shall be opened, and ye shall be as gods, knowing good and evil. 6. And when the woman saw that the tree was good for food, and that it was pleasant to the eyes, and a tree to be desired to make one wise, she took of the fruit thereof, and did eat, and gave also unto her husband with her; and he did eat. 7. And the eyes of them both were opened, and they knew that they were naked; and they sewed fig leaves together, and made themselves aprons. 8. And they heard the voice of the Lord God walking in the garden in the cool of the day: and Adam and his wife hid themselves from the presence of the Lord God amongst the trees of the garden. 9. And the Lord God called unto Adam, and said unto him, Where art thou? 10. And he said, I heard thy voice in the garden and I was afraid, because I was naked; and I hid myself. 11. And he said, Who told thee that thou wast naked? Hast thou eaten of the tree, whereof I commanded thee that thou shouldest not eat? 12. And the man said, The woman whom thou gavest to be with me, she gave me of the tree, and I did eat. 13.And the Lord God said unto the woman, What is this that thou hast done? And the woman said, The serpent beguiled me, and I did eat. 14. And the Lord God said unto the serpent, Because thou hast done this, thou art cursed above all cattle, and above every beast of the field; upon thy belly shalt thou go, and dust shalt thou eat all the days of thy life: 15. And I will put enmity between thee and the woman, and between thy seed and her seed; it shall bruise thy head, and thou shalt bruise his heel.

The Lord knows all things: from beginning to end. He gave man choice but knew that man would go astray. God would not let man go from him and therefore made provision to deliver him, from the foundation of the world. The preparation for a Saviour was already made and it did not take God any time to utter the words of deliverance from the powers of darkness: *"I will put enmity between thee and the woman, and between thy seed and her seed; it shall bruise thy head, and thou shalt bruise his heel"*. The deliverer would come who would bring man back into fellowship with the Father.

Sin brings more sin. Instead of repenting, the man blamed the woman for his sin, [in fact, he was blaming God for the woman he gave him]; the woman blamed the serpent. God gave man sufficient strength to combat sin. Man was given authority to rule. He was wilful. He had become proud like the devil and wanted to be who God did not create him to be. He believed the lies of the devil and fell under the condemnation of death.

Although man would be restored into fellowship with the Father, there would be a severe price to pay. Sin brought the curse upon the human race. As far as getting things right was concerned, there was little hope because man had taken on the nature of the devil and although God prepared a way to cover man's sin, his heart remained calloused. Burnt offering and sacrifices of animals with much shedding of animal blood could not deliver him from sin and he just provoked the Lord to anger day by

17

day. At times God slew many people as they corrupted themselves. The curse was upon man and he was unable to do right in his own strength. Man had lost the ability to do good and he would have to sweat it out to survive in a world that became sinful and wicked, as he handed over his authority, given to him by God to the devil, by his disobedience. Someone might blame the woman, but God had given the man the rulership. The woman was to be his helper. He was guilty. However, God's great love for man would remedy the situation in due time.

The woman was meant to have her babies beautifully but sin brought the curse of dreadful sorrow in childbirth to name just one of the awful punishments. The serpent's wings were clipped completely. He would lose all his evil and deceitful power. God said it, and it would be so.

What are to learn from this to help us in this sin sick world?

a] Whatever the Word of God says should be obeyed. The Word of God is the voice of God. God is still speaking to people. He is still giving instructions to deliver man from the wiles of the devil. Satan is a liar and a deceiver. He hates man and has set out to destroy him in his fight against God. We must be on our guard at all times. The first couple were not on their guard and they were overcome by the devil.

b] When the Lord has blessed us with his authority we should be careful not to become proud and therefore give place to the devil. *Ephesians 4:27 Neither give place to the devil.*

c] When the Lord points out our sin we should repent

18

immediately and not blame others for our wickedness. Blaming others will not remove the punishment we deserve, and our sin remains. Blaming others is adding sin to sin.

d] Satan does not mind being blamed. His self-given job is to steal, kill and destroy. He hates man with a bitter hatred and he is quite happy to take the blame since this means he has achieved his goal.

The kind of curses meted out to the couple:

Genesis 3:16-24 16.Unto the woman he said, I will greatly multiply thy sorrow and thy conception; in sorrow thou shalt bring forth children; and thy desire shall be to thy husband, and he shall rule over thee. 17. And unto Adam he said, Because thou hast hearkened to the voice of thy wife, and hast eaten of the tree, of which I commanded thee, saying, Thou shalt not eat of it: cursed is the ground for thy sake; in sorrow shalt thou eat of it all the days of thy life; thorns also and thistles shall it bring forth to thee; and thou shalt eat the herb of the field; in the sweat of thy face shalt thou eat bread, till thou return unto the ground, for out of it wast thou taken: for dust thou art, and unto dust shalt thou return. 24. So he drove out the man; and he placed at the east of the garden of Eden Cherubims, and a flaming sword which turned every way, to keep the way of the tree of life.

The woman was not given a chance by the devil to have her babies in peace. The Lord had told them to be fruitful and multiply and replenish the earth. In the devil's evil mind this would have been too good to be so, for her. She fell for his lies and he left her to bear the consequence. That must have been a good laugh for the devil because

19

he knows that the penalty for sin can be very severe. He knows about the flames of hell and the stench of burning suphur.

As for the man, the burden of sin for him and his offspring from then onwards would be unbearably heavy to carry. He would work hard for his living and the earth that the Lord had blessed for him would be cursed and be a burden to him instead of a blessing. That is why we are so tired day by day and find it so hard to stay refreshed in our bodies and mind. Worse than all, man would die, physically and spiritually. He would go back to the dust from whence he was taken. People are dying by the multitudes every day from all sorts of diseases, from wars, from natural disasters, from famines and pestilences, from stress and every evil source there is. Disobedience, rebellion and believing the devil's lies, bring certain destruction and alienation from the presence of the Lord.

FULFILLED: St John 3: 16 For God so loved the world that he gave his only begotten Son that whosoever believeth in him should not perish, but have everlasting life.

What can we learn here?

a] We should obey God rather than the devil.

b] Man was under the condemnation of death when he sinned, and if we do not do what is right in the sight of the Lord, to obey his voice and walk in his ways, we too will be condemned to die. They died physically and spiritually and so will we if we walk in disobedience.

c] We are likely to be plagued with sickness and disease

if we allow ourselves to fall under the curse.

d]   We could be driven out of God's spiritual paradise, and angels will keep us out with the drawn sword [the Word of God], if we make a fool of ourselves and listen to the devil's lies.

e]   We may have to work very hard for very little if we allow the curse to fall upon us.

f]   If we allow ourselves to be driven out of the spiritual garden of Eden [the presence of the Lord] we will be exposed to every evil work of the devil.

It behoves us to obey the voice of the Lord and walk in his holy ways because despite all that has befallen the human race, the Lord continues to love us with an everlasting love, and in lovingkindness he has drawn us to himself. *Jeremiah 31:3 The Lord hath appeared of old unto me, saying, Yea, I have loved thee with an everlasting love: therefore with lovingkindness have I drawn thee.*

Ecclesiastes 12:13-14
Let us hear the conclusion of the whole matter: Fear God and keep his commandments: for this is the whole duty of man. For God shall bring every work into judgment, with every secret thing, whether it be good, or whether it be evil.

CHAPTER 2

GOD'S PLAN FOR MAN AS TYPIFIED IN ABRAHAM

Genesis 22:8   And Abraham said, My son, God will provide himself a lamb for a burnt offering: so they went both of them together.

God ordained that in Abraham all the nations of the world should be blessed. Abraham was a man of faith who had found favour in the sight of the Lord. We are Abraham's seed and heirs according to the promise, if we walk by faith. We will look at how the Father is typified in faithful Abraham.

Genesis 22:1-19   1. And it came to pass after these things, that God did tempt Abraham: and said unto him, Abraham: and he said, Behold, here I am. 2. And he said, Take now thy son, thine only son Isaac, whom thou lovest, and get thee into the land of Moriah; and offer him there for a burnt offering upon one of the mountains which I will tell thee of. 3. And Abraham rose up early in the morning, and saddled his ass, and took two of his young men with him, and Isaac his son, and clave the wood for the burnt offering, and rose up, and went unto the place of which God had told him. 4, Then on the third day Abraham lifted up his eyes and saw the place afar off. 5. And Abraham said unto his young men, Abide ye here with the ass; and I and the lad will go yonder and worship, and come again to you. 6. And Abraham took the wood of the burnt offering, and laid it upon Isaac his son; and he took the fire in his hand, and a knife; and they went both of them together. 7. And Isaac spake unto Abraham his father, and said, My father: and he said, Here am I, my son, And he said, Behold the fire and the wood: but where is the lamb for a burnt offering? 8. And Abraham said, My son, God will provide himself a lamb for a burnt offering: so they went both of them together. 9. And they came to the place which God had told him of; and Abraham built an altar there, and laid the wood in order, and bound Isaac his son, and laid him on the altar upon the wood. 10. And Abraham stretched forth his hand, and took the knife to slay his son. 11. And the angel of the Lord called unto him out of heaven, and said, Abraham, Abraham: and he said, Here am I. 12. And he said, Lay not thine hand upon the lad, neither do thou any thing unto him: for now I know that thou fearest God, seeing thou hast not withheld thy son, thine only son from me. 13. And Abraham lifted up his eyes, and looked, and behold behind him a ram caught in a thicket by his horns; and Abraham went and took the ram, and offered him up for a burnt offering in the stead of his son. 14. And Abraham called the name of that place Jehovahjireh: as it is said to this day, In the mount of the Lord it shall be seen. 15. And the angel of the Lord called unto Abraham out of heaven the second time. 16. And said, By myself have I sworn, saith the Lord, for because thou hast done this thing, and hast not withheld thy son, thine only son: 17. That in blessing I will bless thee, and in multiplying I will multiply thy seed as the stars of the heaven, and as the sand which is upon the sea shore; and thy seed shall possess the gate of his enemies; 18. And in thy seed shall all the nations of the earth be blessed; because thou hast obeyed my voice. 19. So Abraham returned unto his young men, and they rose up and went together to Beersheba; and Abraham dwelt at Beersheba. This is one of the most powerful accounts in the bible of sacrificial giving.

23

Abraham, a man of faith, was asked of God, firstly, to leave his father's house and his kindred and travel out to a land he would show him. Abram [Abraham] did as he was asked of God. *[Genesis 12].*   In process of time the Lord promised Abraham a son, in whom the nations of the earth would be blessed. Abraham laughed because he was one hundred years old and Sarah was ninety years old. *Genesis 17:17   Then Abraham fell upon his face, and laughed, and said in his heart, Shall a child be born unto him that is an hundred years old? And shall Sarah, that is ninety years old, bear?* When Sarah knew of this she also thought it was a big joke. *Genesis 18: 11-14   11. Now Abraham and Sarah were old and well stricken in age; and it ceased to be with Sarah after the manner of women. 12. Therefore Sarah laughed within herself, saying, Afer I am waxed old shall I have pleasure, my lord being old also?   13. And the Lord said unto Abraham, Wherefore did Sarah laugh, saying, Shall I of a surety bear a child, which am old?   14. Is any thing too hard for the Lord? At the time appointed I will return unto thee, according to the time of life, and Sarah shall have a son.*

God is truth, and most faithful and Sarah certainly had her son as the angel had said. Abraham circumcised his son, Isaac [and his older son, Ishmael which he fathered with Hagar the Egyptian maid]. He obeyed the commandments of the Lord. Things seemed to have been going well for Abraham until the day the Lord visited him again with another stiff request. Here he was asked to take his son, the son of the promise, and offer him up as a sacrifice on Mount Moriah. This is a famous mountain: King David bought the threshingfloor here and built an altar unto the Lord to stop the plague which was upon the nation of Israel after he numbered the people and sinned against the Lord *[2 Samuel 24];* It is believed that Solomon's temple was built on Mount Moriah and "On a hill far away stood an old rugged cross" [Christian song] was Mount Moriah. This would make sense, since Abraham typified the Father who sacrificed his one and only Son at the same place. Marvelous!!

The bible says that Abraham rose up early in the morning. This is very important. He did not delay in obeying the word of the Lord. As far as he was concerned obedience is urgent. I am often amazed at the obedience of Isaac. Bible scholars think Isaac might have been, perhaps, about 16 years old. This is not at all certain, but however old he was, he was a good boy who was obedient to his father.

Abraham took a couple of his workers with him, but he left them by the way, once he had viewed the mountain where he was going. Abraham was going to worship God by the sacrifice of his son. What is this? I wonder how many of us as Christians would consider this as worship. We would probably be very fretful and wondering whether the Lord had spoken to us at all. Not so with Abraham. He believed God and proceeded to obey. His willingness showed up because of the time he left to go to Mount Moriah to worship!! He went early in the morning.

We must be careful who we take with us when we are going to worship the Lord with our sacrifice. Some can only go with us so far. When it comes to true worship, many will not be able to go the full way, they must be left by the way and wait until we return. They will not be able to watch us raising the knife, especially when it concerns an only son. Abraham left the possible doubters/faint hearted ones behind and headed for that Mount to offer up his sacrifice. He did not hold back; his whole heart was about obeying the Lord. What a sacrifice!

Isaac did ask his father a very important question whilst on their way. We have the wood, [he was carrying the wood]; we have the knife; we have the fire – Where is the lamb for the burnt offering? Reply by Abraham: God will provide himself a lamb for the burnt offering. [This is one of my favourite scripture verses]. I wonder how Abraham felt when he was asked that question by his son of the promise? I don't know. What I do know is that he did not let that question deter him, he went on to please God.

On arrival at the place of his test, he did all that was required. He bound his son and laid him on the altar. I often wonder what Isaac must have thought. He allowed himself to be bound by his father. What a difference to our children and young people of today and they have never had to go through anything like this! Abraham was just about to kill his son, when the angel of the Lord called out of heaven. What a day that was. Abraham, Abraham, said the angel as he called out from heaven. Do not lay your hand upon the lad. Now I know that you fear the Lord seeing you have not withheld your son from him. Don't do anything to your son. *[Genesis 22:11-12]*. The bible says that the Lord provided a ram which Abraham caught and offered as the burnt offering instead of his son. This is a very touching biblical account of the power of the love of God. May the Lord help us.

God had a special love for Abraham who allowed himself to be used of the Lord to typify what God himself would do. Abraham's mind was made up to make the sacrifice, and God the Father had made his mind up completely to give his only Son to be a sacrifice to deliver the souls of men from the fires of hell and satan's evil kingdom.

St John 3:16 *For God so loved the world, that he gave his only begotten Son, that whosoever believeth in him should not perish, but have everlasting life.*

Abraham went to offer up his only son of the promise. God gave up his only begotten Son at the place Abraham went to offer his son. Abraham called his sacrificial offering "Worship". Praise the Lord. Help us Lord! The angel called out of heaven a second time with these powerful words from the heart of God : ***Genesis 22:16-17*** *16. And said, By myself have I sworn, saith the Lord, for because thou hast done this thing, and hast not withheld thy son, thine only son: 17. That in blessing I will bless thee, and in multiplying I will multiply thy seed as the stars of heaven, and as the sand which is upon the sea shore; and thy seed shall possess the gate of his enemies. 18. And in thy seed shall all the nations of the earth be blessed; because thou hast obeyed my voice.* What a blessing obedience brings. Christians are spiritual children of Abraham when they are faithful and obedient.

In like manner the Father gave Jesus as a sacrifice and after he had obediently accomplished his mission the Father gave him a name that is above every name. Let me quote you from ***Philippians 2:5-11*** *5. Let this mind be in you which was also in Christ Jesus: 6. Who, being in the form of God, thought it not robbery to be equal with God: 7. But made himself of no reputation, and took upon him the form of a servant, and was made in the likeness of men: 8. And being found in fashion as a man, he humbled himself, and became obedient unto death, even the death of the cross. 9. Wherefore God also hath highly exalted him, and given him a name which is above every name: 10. That at the name of Jesus every knee should bow, of things in heaven, and things in earth, and things under the* *earth; 11. And that every tongue should confess that Jesus Christ is Lord, to the glory of God the Father.*

Jesus has the most exalted name in the universe. Satan and his demons must bow at the all-powerful name of Jesus. No one can come to the Father, except through Jesus, the door. Jesus humbled himself, took all the insults sinful man hurled at him, suffered, bled and died alone. He was the perfect sacrifice. Abraham offered up Isaac in a figure, but the Father offered up his only Son in the reality. The Father has committed all things into the hands of the Son. *St John 3:35 The Father loveth the Son, and hath given all things into his hand.* God loved Abraham so much because he exercised the obedience, in a shadow, that his Son would exercise in the reality. Today, whoever wants to go to heaven, must confess the Lordship of the Lord Jesus Christ.

FULFILLED: St John 10:15, 17 15. As the Father knoweth me, even so know I the Father: and I lay down my life for the sheep. 17. Therefore doth my Father love me, because I lay down my life, that I might take it again.

What can we learn from this to help us in our walk with the Lord?

1] We should be prepared to leave our father's house and our kindred when the Lord calls us and we should not look back. Abraham kept his eyes on Mount Moriah. No looking back. *Luke 9:62 And Jesus said unto him, No man, having put his hand to the plough, and looking back, is fit for the kingdom of heaven.*

2] We should rise up early to the call of the Lord, having a deep desire to please him. However great the sacrifice

28

we are called to make, it is an act of worship. This blessed my soul as I studied it. Abraham told his son they were going to worship!!

3]   We should not travel to the Mount of the Lord when we are going to offer our worship [complete sacrifice] with people who do not understand what it is to have the highest level of faith in God.

4]   If we walk in obedience and trust the Lord to bring us through whatever he asks us to do, however difficult it may seem, we will find favour with God and he will promote us to the highest level. Do you want to be called a friend of God? Walk in obedience and trust him to the uttermost. Abraham was called, the friend of God. *James 2:23 And the scripture was fulfilled which saith, Abraham believed God, and it was imputed unto him for righteousness: and he was called the friend of God.*

5]   The Lord will work things in our favour as long as we abide in his will for our lives. Can we see how tender and gentle Isaac was, as he allowed his father to bind him and lay him on the sacrificial altar?

6]   We should hold back nothing from the Lord, however important it may seem to us. The Lord can give us much more than we can ever sacrifice for his glory.

7]   Abraham was elevated by the Lord because he did not withhold his son from the Lord, and the Lord pronounced heaven's blessings upon him and his offspring. *Genesis 22: 17a, 18 17a. That in blessing I will bless thee, and in multiplying I will multiply thy seed as the stars of the heaven, and as the sand which is upon the sea shore... 18. And in thy seed shall all the nations of the earth be*

29

blessed, because thou hast obeyed my voice. We want this kind of blessing. What a blessing! May the Lord enable us to obey his voice.

ONE OF MY MANY TESTIMONIES
Dr Daisy Lake

You will be able to read more testimonies in this book because testimonies glorify God. We can do nothing of ourselves and we only get the victory through our Lord Jesus Christ. I will start with just one of my many testimonies. With Jesus, the Holy Spirit and the angels fighting for me, I have never lost a battle. *1 Corinthians 1:9   God is faithful, by whom ye were called unto the fellowship of his Son Jesus Christ.*

I have learned to be obedient to the Lord. He is always right and whatever he tells me to do, I do it gladly because it always brings positive results.

Psalms 27:1   The Lord is my light and my salvation, whom shall I fear? The Lord is the strength of my life, of whom shall I be afraid?

I went to bed as usual and was sleeping well, until the demons came into my bedroom. I had said my prayers and done my scripture reading and studies before laying down to sleep. The devil is no respecter of persons; he will always try out his wickedness even when he knows he cannot win. My beautiful sleep was disturbed by the most awful presence and I began to struggle whilst being half asleep. I struggled to call upon the Lord. I managed to call upon the name of Jesus and felt that I had been loosed. I got up and began to minister the word of God. I was very angry at the devil and his demons. They had no

30

right in my home; I am a child of God, born of the water, the Spirit and the blood of Jesus. I called upon the name of the Lord and felt the anointing of the Lord come upon me. The Holy Ghost began to minister to me by the word of God. I obeyed the voice of the Lord and quoted scripture verses and whole chapters of the bible in the power of the Holy Ghost. I did not know I knew so much of the word of God because scripture on top of scripture came to mind. I lifted up the name of Jesus, in holy anger and told the demons to go. What seemed like a pole or rod dropped somehow in front of me and the word from *Isaiah 59:19* came to mind *[When the enemy shall come in like a flood, the Spirit of the Lord shall lift up a standard against him]* and I took hold of the authority the Lord gave me and drove out the demons by the power of the word of God. "Get out in the name of Jesus", I said. "Leave now in Jesus' name".

I felt when the evil powers left the room and the place became peaceful. It was war that night. In fact it was in the early hours of the morning. I had the victory in the mighty name of Jesus. Satan and his demons came out against me because I was doing a lot of warfare work for the Lord, delivering the souls of men from the clutches of the devil. The demons were fighting back, but Jesus Christ is Lord and as long as we walk in his will, no evil shall befall us. Jesus told us in *Luke 10:19 Behold, I give unto you power to tread on serpents and scorpions, and over all the power of the enemy, and nothing shall by any means hurt you.* I obeyed the voice of the Lord and got the victory. When the demons left, I just praised the Lord and gave him all the glory. The devil and his demons are liars. Stand your ground against the works of darkness when satan and his demons come against you. Do what the word says, command them to leave you in the name of

Jesus. They have to go because the Holy Spirit and the angels of the Lord will fight for you. You must believe this. It is the truth. You cannot lose a battle as long as you stand upon the word of God.

Are you having problems with your sleep at night, or in the early hours of the morning? Do what I did. Drive the demons away in the name of the Lord Jesus Christ. It works. Then praise the Lord.

Blessings.

CHAPTER 3

JOSEPH A TYPE OF DELIVERER

If I may, I will bring to your mind briefly the story of Joseph how God used him to be a mighty deliverer of his people. [Please read through *Genesis 37; and chapters 39-50* –[Read these in your own time and at your own pace].

Genesis 46:1-7 1. *And Israel took his journey with all that he had, and came to Beersheba, and offered sacrifices unto the God of his father Isaac. 2. And God spake unto Israel in the visions of the night, and said, Jacob, Jacob. And he said, Here am I. 3. And he said, I am God, the God of thy father: fear not to go down into Egypt; for I will there make of thee a great nation: 4. I will go down with thee into Egypt; and I will also surely bring thee up again: and Joseph shall put his hand upon thine eyes. 5. And Jacob rose up from Beersheba: and the sons of Israel carried Jacob their father, and their little ones, and their wives, in the wagons which Pharaoh had sent to carry him. 6. And they took their cattle, and their goods, which they had gotten in the land of Canaan, and came into Egypt, Jacob, and all his seed with him. 7. His sons, and his sons' sons with him, his daughters, and his son's daughters, and all his seed brought he with him into Egypt.*

Jacob [Israel] had twelve sons by his wives Rachel and Leah and their maidservants. Jacob earned his wives whilst he served his uncle Laban in Padanaram. Jacob loved Rachel and served his uncle seven years for her.

However, according to their custom the older daughter should first be married so Laban, by trickery, gave Jacob the older daughter Leah after the seven years, instead of Rachel. Jacob had to serve another seven years for Rachel whom he loved dearly.

Leah, being fertile was bearing children, but Rachel, was barren. Rachel was deeply distressed because she was not able to bless Jacob with children. The Lord showed her mercy and opened her womb. The first son she bore for Jacob was called Joseph. She died during childbirth of her second son, Benjamin. Jacob loved Joseph very much because he was the son of his old age, and perhaps also, because his mother was Rachel. What Jacob did, which we should be careful not to do as parents, was show favouritism. He made Joseph a coat of many colours and his brothers viewed him with jealousy. As if his father's partiality was not enough, Joseph began to have dreams which suggested that he would rise above his brothers and even his parents. I believe his parents gave deep thought to his dreams, although on one occasion his father rebuked him. *Genesis 37:8-11 8. And his brethren said to him, Shalt thou indeed reign over us? Or shall thou indeed have dominion over us? And they hated him yet the more for his dreams, and for his words. 9. And he dreamed yet another dream, and told it his brethren, and said, Behold, I have dreamed a dream more; and, behold, the sun and the moon and the eleven stars made obeisance to me. 10. And he told it to his father, and to his brethren: and his father rebuked him, and said unto him, What is this dream that thou hast dreamed? Shall I and thy mother and thy brethren indeed come to bow down ourselves to thee to the earth? 11. And his brethren envied him; but his father observed the saying.*

The record says that one day Jacob sent Joseph to see how his brothers were doing. They had gone to look after the animals. After some searching Joseph found them with the help and direction of a man he met during his search. The bible says that when they saw their brother coming their hatred got the better of them and they determined within themselves that they would kill him. The bitterness and hatred was murder itself. By the time Joseph had got to them they had settled it in their hearts what they would do. They would kill him, throw him into a nearby pit and say to their father that an evil beast had slain him. However, Reuben, the older brother pleaded for young Joseph that they should not kill him but cast him into a pit in the wilderness. They stripped him of his coat of many colours ['jealousy coat'] and threw him into the dry pit. Reuben was not there at the time. Their seared conscience was not a problem to them because they then sat down to have their meal. Whilst eating they saw some Ishmeelite salesmen on their way to Egypt with their spices. Judah, in order to deliver the boy out of the hands of his other brothers suggested that they should sell him to the Ishmeelites. This they did and Joseph was taken down to Egypt. When Reuben came and saw that the lad was not in the pit he was shocked and tore his garment. What would they tell their father who loved the boy with such deep love? They would kill a kid of the goats and dip Joseph's coat in the blood which would suggest a wild beast had slain him and they would take it to their father.

When they got home without Joseph and showed their father the coat, he was convinced that the lad been killed by an evil animal, and Jacob mourned for the boy and could not be comforted. The Lord had allowed Joseph to be where he wanted him, in Egypt, even in these adverse circumstances. God had made a promise to Abraham that although his offspring would be strangers in a foreign land where they would be afflicted, he would bring them out with great substance. *[Genesis 15:13-16]*. Joseph had some rough times down there. Obviously, he had lost his family, at least for a time. He was sold to Potiphar, whose wife had him imprisoned because he refused her sinful advances but the Lord was with righteous Joseph and blessed him even in the prison house, so that the keeper of the prison placed Joseph over all the prisoners. There, he interpreted the dreams of two of Pharaoh's servants who were in the prison with him and the interpretations were right. The butler was restored to his job at the palace and the baker was beheaded in accordance with Joseph's interpretation.

The Lord was watching and taking care of Joseph. When Pharaoh had two dreams in the same night, that he could not interepret, neither could any of his magicians or sorcerers, the butler remembered that Joseph had interpreted his dream and that of the baker and he told this to Pharaoh who called for Joseph. God was bringing Joseph to the place where he needed him to be to deliver his people. Joseph came in to Pharaoh but reminded him that it was God who interpreted dreams and would give him the answer he needed. The two dreams meant the same thing. There would be seven years of plenty in Egypt followed by seven years of severe famine *[Genesis 41]*. When Pharaoh saw that Joseph had given him the answer to his dreams and had suggested that he should get someone to organise and store up provision against the seven years of famine, Pharaoh decided that Joseph was the best person for the job. Joseph was there and then elevated to the position of Prime Minister of Egypt. He was next in command to Pharaoh. The seven years of plenty was over and the seven years of famine came upon

Egypt. However, the famine was in all the then known world. Things were very thin in Joseph's father's house 'back home'. Israel heard that there was corn [food] in Egypt and he sent his sons down to Egypt to buy corn. Things went well for them, but it was only a matter of time before Joseph, who recognised his brothers, would begin to work out ways and means to get his father down to Egypt. Joseph accused them of being spies and had them tell him the full story of his father's house and how Joseph 'was not'. He enquired if his father was still alive. He longed to see his young brother Benjamin, whom his father had refused to send to Egypt with the older brothers. Joseph spoke to them roughly and bound and kept Simeon in Egypt until such time as they brought Benjamin down. Obviously, Jacob remembered what had happened when he sent Joseph to them. The famine got more and more severe and Israel had no option but to send the boy with them, because they were forbidden by Joseph to come again to buy food unless they brought Benjamin down with them. Judah said he would be surety for the boy. They bought food all right and started their journey back home, except that Joseph had had his special cup put in Benjamin's sack, and got his servant to follow behind them and search the sacks for his cup. Of course, the cup was in Benjamin's sack. Joseph ordered that Benjamin be brought back to him.

After all this, Joseph broke down and wept. He told them who he was and ordered his servants to lay on a banquet for his brothers, and he let everyone know that they were his brothers. He became very excited and told Pharaoh about his father and that he wished to see him and to have him to be with him in Egypt. The Lord was working in Joseph's behalf and Pharaoh gave chariots to go and bring Israel and his whole family down to Egypt. God was working his purposes out. The Lord's people, in accordance with God's promise, must be delivered and what started out very badly, turned out to be a blessing because God was in it. If God is in your life today, your problems will turn out to be a blessing in the name of Jesus.

Genesis 50:19 But as for you, ye thought evil against me; but God meant it unto good, to bring to pass, as it is this day to save much people alive.

Israel was very excited and went down to Egypt in the chariots which Pharaoh sent for him and his family. All sixty six of them travelled down to Egypt. Joseph asked of Pharaoh that his father's house dwelt in Goshen because they had many animals. They had everything they needed during the time of the famine and all went well for them as long as Israel was alive. However, the time came that Jacob [Israel] died. The brothers thought that Joseph would turn against them because of what they had done to him. Not so, at all. Joseph feared God and reminded his brothers that what had happened was in the will of the Lord. What is happening to you shall turn out to be a blessing, in the name of Jesus.

Goshen was going to be a very notable place in time. God had them to be there because the destroying angel would move against the Egyptians but Goshen would be covered by the blood. Be happy in your Goshen. It is your place of deliverance.

FULFILLED: St Matthew 26:14-16 14. Then one of the twelve, called Judas Iscariot, went unto the chief priests. 15. And said unto them, What will ye give me, and I will deliver him unto you? And they covenanted with him for thirty pieces of silver. [Joseph was sold and became

Israel's deliverer. Jesus was sold and became mankind's deliverer].

What can we learn from all this

1] As parents we should not show partiality. We should love all our children. If we do not, we can create hatred amongst them and cause terrible things to happen, especially when they are not saved.

2] We should be careful not to allow jealousy to get the better of us. We should repent and get every bit of hatred and jealousy out of our hearts because this is murder.

3] Be the one who will rescue the brethren from the envy and hatred of the jealous saints. The Father loves all of us and we are all wearing the coat of many colours.

4] The brothers sold Joseph to the Ishmeelites who sold him to Potiphar in Egypt. This stumbling block was a stepping stone to fulfil God's promise to Abraham. Joseph would be a deliverer. God's people would be delivered by his hand and God would bring good out of evil.

5] Joseph's brothers did not tell the truth to Jacob, but they had to tell the truth to Joseph. Behold your sin will find you out. *[Numbers 32:23]*. God will expose our wickedness if we do not repent.

6] Despite all that befell Joseph, he was elevated to the place where God created him to be. He was second in command in Egypt. No one can stop you from being whom God created you to be if you will live in harmony with the word of God. Joseph was a righteous man.

7] Israel was re-united with his beloved son, Joseph, in accordance with the will of God. Keep praying and trusting the Lord, your righteous dreams will become true.

8] The Lord used Joseph to bring the Israelites into Egypt to fulfil his plan for them and to bring about a greater deliverance which would typify the coming of our Lord Jesus Christ to deliver man from satan and the host of darkness.

9] It is only a matter of time that the blood of the sacrificial lamb would be shed to protect the Israelite homes from the destroying angel and God's people would come forth with great substance to serve their God. You will be delivered from every evil situation as long as you are in the will and plan of God for your life. All your enemies will be disgraced and you will be the victor whom God will promote for his glory.

Joseph was delivered from the evil schemes of his brothers and below is a testimony from a sister who was delivered from her sickness. This goes to say that whatever the adverse situation, God is well able to deliver you.

MY TESTIMONY OF DELIVERANCE
Sister E

My condition needed deliverance from the Lord. God delivers in so many different ways and satan and his demons will do all they can to divert you from receiving help from the Lord. Satan will give you every reason why you should not attend a Holy Ghost fire-powered church, where God can meet your needs. Do not listen to the lies of the devil. Satan knows how to run evil diseases through families, but God knows how to stop these and break the curses, if you will believe.

The demons who control the gateway of certain diseases are not easily moved; it takes the anointing to break these yokes which often run through families over generations. However, Jesus' power and anointing is available to destroy every heartache, pain and suffering.

I am from a family of diabetics. My mother had died from the disease and my younger sister also died from the disease when she was only 51 years old. At the age of 41 years the doctors diagnosed that I, too, had the deadly disease. Obviously, I was very worried and thought I would probably die from it as well. As the years went by, my condition worsened and my eyesight became very poor. I went to the opticians who sent me to the doctor. I was already under the treatment of the hospital doctors. Tests were carried out and glaucoma was diagnosed.

As a qualified nurse working on hospital wards over many years, I have seen the result of certain diseases. The drugs I was given for the glaucoma and for the diabetes did not seem to help, and the doctors feared what I feared, that I may end up becoming blind.

One of my sisters had been very ill for nearly nineteen years. She had had some six operations and was bound to a wheelchair. She was in constant pain and the doctors could do no more for her.

She was listening to a radio broadcast one Sunday morning by Apostle Lake. She mentioned, as she preached the word of God, that there were some of the listeners who were so ill they were as good as dead. She said there was a crusade to be held where people could come and have their needs met by the Lord Jesus Christ. My sister was taken there and received prayer. She later attended one of the church services where Apostle Lake and other ministers prayed for her, spoke the word of God over her life and pleaded the blood of Jesus. She received a miracle at the service and she told me what happened, which I will state briefly: My sister told me that she felt hands physically operating on her. The power of God had thrown her on the floor after she had been prayed for and whilst she was on the floor, she felt herself being operated on, and parts being put in her body. Whatever happened, when she got up off that floor, she was completely healed. A notable miracle had taken place.

"Come and receive your healing", my sister said. I was sceptical and would not attend the meeting for a while. However, one Sabbath, on my way to work, I thought about getting healed. I turned my car around and went to the church. Prayer time came and I went up for prayer. Apostle Lake prayed for me and pleaded the blood of Jesus. I had never experienced anything like that before. I was attending one of the mainstream churches where this was not done. However, I just needed to be healed. Apostle Lake told me to go back to the doctors and return with my testimony. I did as she said. The doctors examined me and wondered what had happened.

Remembering that the drugs were no longer working, they asked me what had taken place in my life. I told them that I had received prayer for my condition. They told me the glaucoma had improved very much and the diabetes was under control. I was relieved, and went back to the church with my testimony. Apostle Lake said that God did not do half jobs; she needed to hear that I was completely healed. She prayed for me again whilst the church pleaded the blood of Jesus. I have never seen nor heard anything like that anywhere else, but it surely works. Apostle Lake told me to go back to the hospital for my check up and come back with my testimony.

My next check up was six months away. I went to the hospital at the appointed time and had the tests done as usual. The doctors seemed puzzled. The glaucoma had disappeared, my sight was perfect; I did not need glasses any more and there was no more diabetes. I was overjoyed. I went back to the church and testified of God's miracle working power and we all rejoiced and gave God thanks for his wonderful Son Jesus Christ, and for his precious blood.

Satan was upset. The devil was not very happy about my deliverance and decided to attack me again: I was driving to work in the normal way but found that I was not seeing properly. I managed to drive to the house of the patient I was going to see. [I am a district nurse]. My sight became so bad that my husband had to come and take me home.

I went back to the church and told my problem to Pastor Judy Fullerton. Pastor Judy and Evangelist Blake prayed for me. They pleaded the blood of Jesus over my condition, ministering to me with all their hearts. The power of the Lord threw me on the floor; the Lord dealt with me whilst I was on the floor and when I got up I was completely healed. My sight had returned and today I can see clearly, without the use of glasses. The medical profession is wonderful, I am a part of it, but they could not deny that something outside their understanding had taken place in my life. The Lord Jesus Christ had healed me completely, praise his wonderful name. I thank God for his miracle working power. I thank him for the wonder working power in the blood of Jesus Christ and I can recommend Jesus to meet any need anyone has. About the blood of Jesus: It is certainly most powerful and the devil cannot handle it.

Prayer is powerful and if you have a deadly disease or a problem no one else can solve, why not try Jesus? He will fix it for you; he will never let you down.

CHAPTER 4

MOSES AND DAVID HAD THE REVELATION OF THE FIRST COMING OF THE SAVIOUR

If Jesus is coming again, it means he has come before and we will look at how the Lord revealed the first coming of the Saviour to the patriarchs Moses and David. The word of God is the truth.

MOSES
Deuteronomy 18:15-22   15. The Lord thy God will raise up unto thee a Prophet from the midst of thee, of thy brethren, like unto me; unto him ye shall hearken;   16. According to all that thou desiredst of the Lord thy God in Horeb in the day of the assembly, saying, Let me not hear again the voice of the Lord my God, neither let me see this great fire any more, that I die not.   17. And the Lord said unto me, They have well spoken that which they have spoken.   18. I will raise them up a Prophet from among their brethren, like unto thee, and will put my words in his mouth; and he shall speak unto them all that I shall command him.   19.And it shall come to pass, that whosoever will not hearken to my words which he shall speak in my name, I will require it of him.   20. But the prophet, which shall presume to speak a word in my name, which I have not commanded him to speak, or that shall speak in the name of other gods, even that prophet shall die.   21. And if thou say in thine heart, How shall we know the word which the Lord hath not spoken?   22. When a prophet speaketh in the name of the Lord, if the thing follow not, nor come to pass, that is the thing which

the Lord hath not spoken, but the prophet hath spoken it presumptuously: thou shalt not be afraid of him.

Here the patriarch Moses spoke to his people from the mouth of the Lord that the Lord would raise up a Prophet from amongst them, like unto himself. However, the word says the Prophet would not come from the tribe of Levi. In the fullness of time this Prophet [Jesus] came from the tribe of Juda. *[Hebrews 7:14].*

Moses warned the people that when the Lord had brought them into the land which he promised them they should be careful not to practice the ways of the heathen which the Lord drove out of the land. They should be careful not to be observer of times; they should not consult with familiar spirits, wizards/witches or necromancers and they should not use divination; simply, they should not involve themselves in the occult. How dangerous is occultism? God hates it and drove out those people who practiced occultism and gave their land to his people. Occultism is equal to idolatry because it is worship of satan and his evil demons. *Deuteronomy 18:13 Thou shalt be perfect with the Lord thy God.* God's people are commanded by God to be perfect and should not be like the people of the world, whose works he hates.

At this point, Moses prophesied that the Lord would raise them up a Prophet like unto himself. Moses was a deliverer who brought them up out of the land of Egypt. He was the deliverer/prophet under the Old Covenant, [the shadow] but he told them that there would be another Prophet like him [another Deliverer/Prophet] to whom they should listen. Moses reminded them of the day the Lord met with them in Horeb when the power and glory was so much that they requested that Moses spoke to the

Lord on their behalf. To this the Lord agreed and promised to raise them up a Prophet from among them, like Moses; he would put his word in that Prophet's mouth, and he shall speak unto them *all that I shall command him [verse 18].* Whosoever did not obey the word the Lord commanded by that Prophet, God would require it of that person. In *verse 19,* I believe the Lord was speaking of the false prophets then and now. We have been taught here how to recognise those false prophets and we have many of them in these last and final days. We can tell the true prophet, says the Lord. If the word they have spoken in the name of the Lord comes to pass, we know they are the true prophets, but the words of the false prophets will not come to pass. Let us keep our ears and eyes open and be wise. Listen carefully to what these latter day prophets say in the name of Jesus and match their words up with the word of God; the scriptures. Open your eyes and watch to see if their words come to pass. If their words spoken in the name of the Lord do not come to pass, they are liars, do not believe them. Another point of note: God does not want anyone to worship false gods. Hear what he says here: *Verse 20:* ....or that shall speak in the name of other gods, even that prophet shall die. What about all these false gods that have filled out the nation? and the people who speak in their names. A man of one of the false gods told me on one occasion that if he worshipped his god, he will give him what he needs. Surely, he was speaking in the name of another god. Now, Jesus the Prophet has been raised up from amongst Moses' brethren and these false prophets are not hearkening to his word. Under the New Covenant brought in by Jesus at his first coming, we are no longer walking in the flesh by works but in the spirit by faith. Therefore, these false prophets have died spiritually. As the Lord's people, we should pray that the Lord will open the eyes of these idolaters that they may see Jesus. The systems of the world have embraced idolatry as another way to the Lord, but it is clear that Jesus does not want demon worship. Idolatry is demon worship. *Exodus 20:3-4 3. Thou shalt have no other gods before me. 4. Thou shalt not bow down thyself before them, nor serve them: for I the Lord thy God am a jealous God, visiting the iniquity of the fathers upon the children unto the third and fourth generation of them that hate me.* Idol worship is seen as iniquity by the Lord and there is a negative visitation by the Lord upon those who serve other gods. The God of the bible is a jealous God and woe be unto the nations that embrace idolatry.

DAVID

Psalm 22:1-20 1.My God, my God, why hast thou forsaken me? why art thou far from helping me and from the words of my roaring? 2. O my God, I cry in the daytime, but thou hearest not; and in the night season, and am not silent. 3. But thou art holy, O thou that inhabitest the praises of Israel. 4. Our fathers trusted in thee: they trusted, and thou didst deliver them. 5. They cried unto thee, and were delivered: they trusted in thee, and were not confounded. 6. But I am a worm, and no man; a reproach of men, and despised of the people. 7. All they that see me laugh me to scorn; they shoot out the lip, they shake the head, saying, 8. He trusted on the Lord that he would deliver him; let him deliver him, seeing he delighted in him. 9. But thou art he that took me out of the womb: thou didst make me hope when I was upon my mother's breasts. 10. I was cast upon thee from the womb: thou art my God from my mother's belly. Be not far from me; for trouble is near; for there is none to help. 12. Many bulls have compassed me: strong bulls of Bashan have beset me round. 13. They gaped upon me with their mouths, as a ravening and a roaring lion. 14. I am poured out like water, and all my bones are out of joint: my heart is like wax; it is melted in the midst of my bowels. 15. My strength is dried up like a potsherd; and my tongue cleaveth to my jaws; and thou hast brought me into the dust of death. 16. For dogs have compassed me: the assembly of the wicked have inclosed me: they pierced my hands and my feet. 17. I may tell all my bones: they look and stare upon me. 18. They part my garments among them, and cast lots upon my vesture. 19. But be not thou far from me, O Lord: O my strength, haste thee to help me. 20. Deliver my soul from the sword; my darling from the power of the dog.

The patriarch David, like Moses, prophesied of the first coming of the Lord. David foresaw the suffering Jesus would undergo. He saw Jesus' agony and the insults he would suffer at the hands of sinful men. He had revealed to him how Jesus would be pierced in his hands and feet and how his enemies would part his garments amongst themselves.

St John 19:23-24 23. Then the soldiers, when they had crucified Jesus, took his garments, and made four parts, to every soldier a part; and also his coat: now the coat was without seam, woven from the top throughout. 24. They said therefore among themselves, Let us not rend it, but cast lots for it, whose it shall be: that the scripture might be fulfilled, which saith, They parted my raiment among them, and for my vesture they did cast lots. These things therefore the soldiers did. Yes, prophecy was fulfilled.

Matthew 27:39-43 39. And they that passed by reviled him, wagging their heads. 40. And saying, Thou that

49

destroyest the temple, and buildest it in three days, save thyself. If thou be the Son of God, come down from the cross. 41. Likewise also the chief priests mocking him, with the scribes and elders, said, 42. He saved others; himself he cannot save. If he be the King of Israel, let him now come down from the cross, and we will believe him. He trusted in God, let him deliver him now, if he will have him; for he said, I am the Son of God.

Jesus came, suffered, bled and died at the hands of wicked men. Satan and his demons looked on in glee, not knowing that Jesus, through the sacrifice of himself, had overthrown his wicked kingdom and had delivered man from death and hell. I believe that if satan and his emissaries had any idea whatsoever of the result of Christ's death on that cross, they would not have deceived man into crucifying Jesus. The devil and his demons have forever lost the battle and the gates of hell shall never prevail against God's church, the people he has saved, and will continue to save, from the devil's corrupted kingdom. Satan used the religious leaders of the day to scoff at the precious Lord hanging on that cross. They mocked and spoke some very painful words in the ears of the Son of God: he bore it all alone. David saw them in his prophetic message as bulls of Bashan. He saw Jesus feeling as one in the mouth of lions, being compassed by dogs; with his strength being dried up. This is only a portion of the heavy price the Lord has paid for our sins, and indeed for the sins of the whole world. *God so loved the world, that he gave his only begotten Son, that whosoever believeth in him should not perish, but have everlasting life: [St John 3:16];* a life that lasts for ever. O, the great love that the Father has bestowed upon us that we should be called the sons of God. *[1 John 3:1].*

FULFILLED: St John 14:23-24 23. Jesus answered and said unto him, If a man love me, he will keep my words; and my Father will love him, and we will come unto him, and make our abode with him. 24. He that loveth me not keepeth not my sayings: and the word which ye hear is not mine, but the Father's which sent me.

Matthew 27:46 And about the ninth hour Jesus cried with a loud voice, saying, Eli, Eli, lama sabachthani? That is to say, My God, my God, why hast thou forsaken me?

What great truth is revealed here?

1] That these two great patriarchs/prophets spoke from the mouth of God.

2] How can we be sure that they spoke the truth? We are sure that they spoke the truth because the prophecies came to pass. We would know they were not of the truth if the prophecies did not come to pass. **Deuteronomy 18:22** *When a prophet speaketh in the name of the Lord, if the thing follow not, nor come to pass, that is the thing which the Lord hath not spoken, but the prophet hath spoken it presumptuously: thou shalt not be afraid of him.* About the first coming of the Lord? Jesus came, yes he came in fulfilment of prophecy, the first time, to redeem man from the power of the devil.

MY TESTIMONY
OF GOD'S MIGHTY HAND OF
DELIVERANCE. HE SAVED MY LIFE
by Sister P

I just have to give my testimony of how God saved my life. He delivered me from death and I thank him with all my heart. Now read on:

As far as I was concerned, it was just another morning when I fasted and prayed in my bedroom. I prayed on the subject of faith and the word of God dropped into my spirit: *Luke 8:47-48 47. And when the woman saw that she was not hid, she came trembling, and falling down before him, she declared unto him before all the people for what cause she had touched him, and how she was healed immediately. 48. And he said unto her, Daughter, be of good comfort; thy faith hath made thee whole; go in peace.* This was all about the woman who had an issue of blood for twelve years, and who had pressed her way through the crowd to touch Jesus. Immediately she touched him she was healed. As I meditated on the scripture I fell asleep. However, I was awakened by the voice of my daughter calling out, "Gary, what are you doing here?" I got out of my bed and went into the passage. I then said to my daughter, "Why did you let him in; you know he is mentally ill?" At this point my daughter went into the bathroom and telephoned her dad who was out at that time. He told her to call the police.

Gary then went into my daughter's bedroom and began to look at some photographs but God let me notice a knife in his hand. I thought of running out of the house, but somehow I quickly went back to my room and locked the door thinking I would be safe there. This was not to be so because he came to the door and tried to force himself in. I did all I could to push the door against him; his strength was more than mine. When he saw that the door was not opening for him, he kicked it in and entered the room. I was very frightened. He jumped up on my bed with the knife in his hand and began to stab at me. He stabbed me twice on my left breast and continued to stab at me. I moved around the room as I tried to escape the knife but he did all he could to try and slash my throat. I was terrified and shouted out the name of Jesus. Jesus, Jesus, Jesus, help me, help me!! To God be all the glory he missed my throat every time. I shouted out: "The blood of Jesus, the blood of Jesus, the blood of Jesus". When I called on the name of Jesus and pleaded the blood of Jesus he backed off for a little while but came back with all his strength. He gave me two stab wounds in my stomach and the blood gushed out. By this time there was blood everywhere. I was still trying to dodge him and I fell down because there were things around my room. I fell on my hands and he stooped down and gave me a stab with all his might in my back. By then I had made up my mind that I would die so I just kept on pleading the blood of Jesus and calling on Jesus to have mercy on me.

There was no mercy here, Gary was determined to kill me. There were stab wounds also on my legs and shoulder but I cannot remember when he gave me those. I was too distressed and bleeding too much to remember this. However, I kept pleading the blood of Jesus in my semi-dazed condition and I can remember that he became very confused as I shouted, "The blood of Jesus, the blood of Jesus, the blood of Jesus". He then began to cut up my clothes. God is so faithful. As he continued to cut up my clothes, I heard the voice of the Lord. It said, "Run now". I ran towards the door but because there was so much blood on my hands, my finger slipped. Apparently, he had locked the door when he came into the room. I might have been able to open the door had it not been for the blood on my fingers. I kept on pleading the blood of Jesus and crying out to the Lord Jesus to help me. "Help me Jesus, help me Jesus". Miraculously, the door began to open slowly and the police came in, thank God. They told him to drop the knife and he ran through the door and out of the house. When the door opened I went out and sat on the step; a neighbour came out and gave me a towel to put under my breast because I was bleeding very heavily.

The ambulance arrived. They took me downstairs and into the ambulance. I was aware of how serious my condition was and I repented. I asked the Lord to forgive me of any sins that may be in my life; I asked him to save me from death so that I can be with my two young children. I prayed and prayed. When I got to the hospital I was bleeding very badly. They did all the normal tests and thanks be to God who gives us the victory through our Lord Jesus Christ, there was nothing to find. No vital organ was damaged, except for the many knife wounds which would heal, by the mercies of the Lord. However, the doctors told me that the knife wound to my back was a serious one and if the knife had gone down a bit further I would have died.

The story has not yet ended. The devil and his evil demons were not prepared to give up. They were bent on killing me, but Jesus Christ is Lord and he had given his angels charge over me to keep me in all my ways: my blood count kept falling to an all-time low. I had to remain in hospital a little longer until they had done several tests to try and find out why, but the Lord was with me. With the prayers of God's wonderful people, my blood count began to go up. It was only another couple of days when I was allowed to go home. Praise the Lord. I say with all my heart, "Thank you Jesus my Lord for saving my life". I am still numbered with the living.

AN IMPORTANT POINT OF NOTE: When I got to the hospital I asked the nurse to ring Dr Lake for me and let her know I was in hospital. I wrote her name and phone number on a piece of paper because by this time I was very weak indeed. Dr Lake managed to speak to a member of my family who told her what had happened. I believe in the power of prayer and I know Dr Lake would ring all whom she could get in touch with, and ask them to pray about my condition. The saints began to pray from the time they had the news and Dr Lake rang me almost every day and prayed for me.

To God be all the glory and praise, today I am well and doing fine, all because of the mercies of God and the power of the blood of Jesus and the authority in the name of Jesus. Satan and his demons were again defeated. I am alive to be with my two young children, Lee and Z'hane. I want to say a special Thank You to Dr Lake and all the ministers and saints everywhere who have prayed for me. To Jesus be all the thanks and praise in the entire universe; may he be forever glorified. Thank You Jesus, my Lord.

I hope you never find yourself in the situation I was in, but in whatsoever situation you find yourself, call upon the name of the Lord. Cry out to the Lord for help, he will never forsake you. I was cornered by the devil and his evil demons, mine was a near death experience but Jesus brought me out. If you are not praying, learn to pray. Learn to call upon the name of Jesus because you do not know when you will be in a desperate condition where only God can help you. If you are not saved, get saved so you can learn how to call upon the Lord for his help.

Joel 2:32 And it shall come to pass that whosoever shall call on the name of the Lord, shall be delivered.....

CHAPTER 5

THE PROPHETS FORETOLD CHRIST'S FIRST COMING

The patriarchs foretold the first coming of the Lord, and so did the prophets. When the prophecy comes to pass we know it is the truth; it is from God. Jesus did come into the world to die in order to redeem a lost world, over two thousand years ago. He died for you and he died for me.

ISAIAH
Isaiah 9:2-7 2. The people that walked in darkness have seen a great light: they that dwell in the land of the shadow of death, upon them hath the light shined. 3. Thou hast multiplied the nation, and not increased the joy: they joy before thee according to the joy in harvest, and as men rejoice when they divide the spoil. 4. For thou hast broken the yoke of his burden, and the staff of his shoulder, the rod of his oppressor, as in the day of Midian. 5. For every battle of the warrior is with confused noise, and garments rolled in blood; but this shall be with burning and fuel of fire. 6. For unto us a child is born, unto us a Son is given: and the government shall be upon his shoulder: and his name shall be called Wonderful, Counsellor, The mighty God, The everlasting Father, The Prince of Peace. 7. Of the increase of his government and peace there shall be no end, upon the throne of David, and upon his kingdom, to order it, and to establish it with judgment and with justice from henceforth even for ever. The zeal of the Lord of hosts will perform this.

We are talking about the first coming of the Lord as

foretold by the prophets. Isaiah received revelation from God and was God's mouthpiece in this regard. At the time Isaiah gave this prophecy the Israelites were in terrible darkness as regards the things of God. There was much idolatry until Hezekiah began to reign. Isaiah was the prophet who sought the Lord during king Hezekiah's reign. Hezekiah was a righteous king. When he came to the throne the doors of the house of the Lord were closed; the lamps had been put out; burnt offerings had ceased to be offered. The temple was in a bad way, so Hezekiah gave orders to have the house of the Lord reopened and sanctified. *2 Chronicles 29:5, 7, 16. 5. And said unto them, Hear me, ye Levites, sanctify now yourselves, and sanctify the house of the Lord God of your fathers, and carry forth the filthiness out of the holy place. 7. Also they have shut up the doors of the porch, and put out the lamps, and have not burned incense nor offered burnt offerings in the holy place unto the God of Israel. 16. And the priest went into the inner part of the house of the Lord, to cleanse it, and brought out all the uncleanness that they found in the temple of the Lord into the court of the house of the Lord. And the Levites took it, to carry it out abroad into the brook Kidron.*

When Isaiah received the prophecy from the Lord this was the state of the people, and the Lord revealed to Isaiah that there would be One who would come and take the people out of that great darkness; a great light would come unto them. They would come out of the land of the shadow of death as the light shined unto them.

Yes, a child would be born and a Son given, upon whose shoulder the government would be. The nations of the world had been having some evil governments, but there would appear a righteous government under this Son's rulership. Those who needed counsel could go to him. The One coming would be called Wonderful [our God is truly wonderful]; The mighty God [our God is truly mighty - nothing and no one can withstand his might]; the everlasting Father [he would be a Father to the fatherless, and he would always be there when he was needed]; the Prince of Peace [a Prince indeed whose dominion would have no end; whose kingdom would be a kingdom of peace. Peace is so very important to everyone and there would be no end to this government and its peace]. This government would be a just government. Praise the Lord. Did the Prince of Peace come? Yes, he did come and he is coming again.

Isaiah 53:1-7, 10   1. Who hath believed our report? And to whom is the arm of the Lord revealed? 2. For he shall grow up before him as a tender plant, and as a root out of a dry ground: he hath no form nor comeliness; and when we shall see him, there is no beauty that we should desire him. 3.He is despised and rejected of men; a man of sorrows, and acquainted with grief: and we hid as it were our faces from him; he was despised, and we esteemed him not. 4. Surely he hath borne our griefs, and carried our sorrows: yet we did esteem him stricken, smitten of God, and afflicted. 5.But he was wounded for our transgressions, he was bruised for our iniquities: the chastisement of our peace was upon him; and with his stripes we are healed. 6. All we like sheep have gone astray; we have turned every one to his own way; and the Lord hath laid on him the iniquity of us all. 7. He was oppressed, and he was afflicted, yet he opened not his mouth: he is brought as a lamb to the slaughter, and as a sheep before her shearers is dumb, so he openeth not his mouth. 10. Yet it pleased the Lord to bruise him; he hath put him to grief: when thou shalt make his soul an

59

offering for sin, he shall see his seed, he shall prolong his days, and the pleasure of the Lord shall prosper in his hand.

Who has believed the report? the prophet asked. Isaiah foresaw that the Messiah would come and there would be some who would not believe the prophecy. Surely, the Scribes and Pharisees did not believe that a king could come in a manger. Kings are, in the natural, born in palaces, but this was no natural King; he was a supernatural King. He would come in a way in which the poor of this world could identify and have a chance to be saved. Things were really terrible at the time the Lord Jesus came. There were many deaf, dumb, blind and diseased people around who needed help. They would not feel able to go to a palace and seek help, but they could go to Jesus. He walked among them; ate and drank with them. He put everyone at ease so that he could fulfil the mission for which he came into the world – to save sinners and to deliver the hopeless. *Acts 10:38 How God anointed Jesus of Nazareth with the Holy Ghost and with power: who went about doing good, and healing all who were oppressed of the devil; for God was with him.* The poor and helpless ones believed the report. Jesus knew it would be difficult to convince the rich; they have everything; they can pay their way through life.

Isaiah detailed the root of the Christ. He would come from a poor background [a root out of a dry ground]; he would not be what the world would call beautiful. However, he would bear our griefs, carry our sorrows, and there were then, and there are now, multitudes of sorrowful people in this sinful world. He would not be esteemed highly, but the writer beautifully puts it: *"But he was wounded for our transgressions, he was bruised for our iniquity, the chastisement of our peace was upon him and with his stripes we are healed. [verse 5].*

Isaiah gave the prophecy in the present tense because it is as good for us today as it was for the people in Jesus' day. Man had sinned and was like sheep gone astray, but the Lord laid on Jesus the sins of all of us. Praise the Lord.

The prophet explained Jesus' trial, the suffering he would undergo and how he would be silent before his accusers. It pleased the Lord to allow Jesus to suffer because of God's great love for man and Jesus' love and willingness to give his life for us all. Jesus was made an offering for our sins but the pleasure of the Lord would prosper in his hand. He would be victorious, and man would be delivered from the power of sin and satan.

Matthew 27:12-14 *12. And when he was accused of the chief priests and elders, he answered nothing. 13. Then said Pilate unto him, Hearest thou not how many things they witness against thee? 14. And he answered him to never a word; insomuch that the governor marvelled greatly.*

Jesus stood before his accusers and refused to give answers to their accusations. He remained silent.

Isaiah 11:-1-2 *1. And there shall come forth a rod out of the stem of Jesse, and a Branch shall grow out of his roots. 2. And the Spirit of the Lord shall rest upon him, the spirit of wisdom and understanding, the spirit of counsel and might, the spirit of knowledge and of the fear of the Lord.*
Jesus was the Branch that came from the roots of Jesse.

61

The Spirit of the Lord was upon him as witnessed at his baptism. The Spirit of the Lord descended upon him as he came up out of the water. *Mathew 3:16-17 16. And Jesus, when he was baptized, went up straightway out of the water: and, lo, he saw the Spirit of God descending like a dove, and lighting upon him. 17. And lo a voice from heaven, saying, This is my beloved Son, in whom I am well pleased.*

The spirit of wisdom and understanding was upon Jesus in such a way that from the age of twelve he was confounding the doctors of the law in the temple at Jerusalem. Jesus declared this himself when he stated the following: *Luke 4:18 The Spirit of the Lord is upon me, because he hath anointed me to preach the gospel to the poor, he hath sent me to heal the brokenhearted, to preach deliverance to the captives, and recovering of sight to the blind, to set at liberty them that are bruised.*
The spirit of counsel and might was upon Jesus. Might, because none of his adversaries could withstand him. He walked through the midst of some of those who would stone him *[St John 8:59]*. Jesus was mighty to drive out the demons from the oppressed and demonized people. *Mark 5:7-8 7. And cried with a loud voice, and said, What have I to do with thee, Jesus, thou Son of the most high God? I adjure thee by God, that thou torment me not. 8. For he said unto him, Come out of the man, thou unclean spirit.*

The fear of the Father was upon Jesus at all times when he said in the Garden of Gethsemane, *Father, if thou be willing, remove this cup from me; nevertheless, not my will, but thine, be done. [Luke 22:42].*

Isaiah 7:14 Therefore the Lord himself shall give you a

sign; Behold, a virgin shall conceive, and bear a son, and shall call his name Immanuel.

God sent his Son to earth to redeem the human race and to be with us. Jesus spent some three and a half years wearing human flesh, and being with humans to show us how to please the Father and to do his will. The gospel of Matthew reminds us that the Son who was being given to us would be God with us. ***Matthew 1:23*** *Behold a virgin shall be with child, and shall bring forth a son, and they shall call his name Emmanuel, which being interpreted is, God with us.*

FULFILLED: Luke 1:26-35; Luke 2:10-11
Luke 1:26-35 *26. And in the sixth month the angel Gabriel was sent from God unto a city of Galilee, named Nazareth, 27. To a virgin espoused to a man whose name was Joseph, of the house of David; and the virgin's name was Mary. 28. And the angel came in unto her, and said, Hail, thou that art highly favoured, the Lord is with thee: blessed art thou among women. 29. And when she saw him, she was troubled at his saying, and cast in her mind what manner of salutation this should be. 30. And the angel said unto her, Fear not, Mary: for thou hast found favour with God. 31. And, behold, thou shalt conceive in thy womb, and bring forth a son, and shalt call his name JESUS. 32. He shall be great, and shall be called the Son of the Highest: and the Lord God shall give unto him the throne of his father David. 33. And he shall reign over the house of Jacob for ever, and of his kingdom there shall be no end. 34. Then said Mary unto the angel, How shall this be, seeing I know not a man? 35. And the angel answered and said unto her, The Holy Ghost shall come upon thee, and the power of the highest shall overshadow thee, therefore also that holy thing which shall be born of*

thee shall be called the Son of God.

Luke 2:10-11 *10. And the angel said unto them, Fear not: for, Behold I bring you good tidings of great joy, which shall be to all people. 11. For unto you is born this day in the city of David a Saviour, which is Christ the Lord.*

Isaiah was one of the major prophets who went into detail as he prophesied of Christ's humble beginnings, and the sufferings he would undergo in order to bring man out of satan's kingdom; the treatment that would be meted out by the religious leaders, his cruel death, [how he would be treated in the judgment hall and how he would not retaliate or defend himself]; and the rich burial he would receive after the crucifixion.

Matthew 15:7-8 *7. Ye hypocrites, well did Esaias prophecy of you, saying, 8. These people draweth nigh unto me with their mouth, and honoureth me with their lips, but their heart is far from me.*

Luke 2:7 *And she brought forth her firstborn son, and wrapped him in swaddling clothes, and laid him in a manger; because there was no room for them in the inn.*

Matthew 27:12-14 *12. And when he was accused of the chief priests and elders, he answered nothing. 13.Then said Pilate unto him, Hearest thou not how many things they witness against thee? 14. And he answered him to never a word; insomuch that the governor marvelled greatly.*

Luke 23:50-53 *50. And behold, there was a man named Joseph, a counseller; and he was a good man, and a just:*

51. [The same had not consented to the counsel and deed of them]; he was of Arimathea, a city of the Jews; who also himself waited for the kingdom of God. 52. This man went unto Pilate, and begged the body of Jesus. 53. And he took it down, and wrapped it in linen, and laid it in a sepulchre that was hewn in stone, wherein never man before was laid.

Jesus was crucified between outcasts of society, but he received a rich man's burial and so he should; he made all things. He came the first time, suffered, bled and died alone, for you and for me, and he is coming again to reward the faithful.

JEREMIAH
Jeremiah 31:15 *Thus saith the Lord; A voice was heard in Ramah, lamentation, and bitter weeping; Rachel weeping for her children refused to be comforted for her children, because they were not.*

Jeremiah saw in prophecy how the Lord's enemy would attempt to kill Jesus. Satan and his cohorts lived in fear of what God might be doing to destroy his evil kingdom and did all he could think of to ruin God's deliverance of man. The devil was not at all worried that many innocent children would be killed, that many parents would be weeping, as long as he killed Jesus. God foresaw this and had plans for the deliverance of the Christ child. Satan used king Herod, a wicked man to try and effect his purposes, but God moved ahead of him. Our God knows the past, the present and the future, and he had already put his plans in place to protect Jesus. He was born for a purpose and the purpose would be fulfilled. Nothing would be allowed to stop that. All power belongs to our God and he knows how to deliver.

FULFILLED Matthew 2:16-18 16. Then Herod, when he saw that he was mocked of the wise men, was exceeding wroth, and sent forth, and slew all the children that were in Bethlehem, and in all the coasts thereof, from two years old and under, according to the time which he had diligently enquired of the wise men. 17. Then was fulfilled that which was spoken by Jeremy the prophet, saying, 18. In Rama was there a voice heard, lamentation, and weeping, and great mourning, Rachel weeping for her children, and would not be comforted, because they are not.

Yes, evil king Herod worked at destroying the Christ child because the wise men, being warned of God, did not return to him with news about the child. Unfortunately for him, God had commanded Joseph to take the young child and his mother and flee into Egypt. Satan was always about spoiling God's plan for man; he was not successful in the case of Jesus and he will never be successful against God's people.

MICAH

Micah 5:2 But thou, Bethlehem Ephratah, though thou be little among the thousands of Judah, yet out of thee shall he come forth unto me that is to be ruler in Israel; whose goings forth have been from of old, from everlasting. Jesus was born in Bethlehem of Judah. He would proceed from this tribe and he would rule Israel; and not only Israel but the whole world. He has been from everlasting. Jesus laid down his heavenly kingship to come down to earth the first time to bring man up to heaven. He was not just King of the Jews, he is king of Kings and Lord of Lords of the entire universe. He came down low to bring us up high. To Jesus be all the praise and glory.

FULFILLED   Matthew 2:1-2 1. Now when Jesus was born in Bethlehem of Judaea in the days of Herod the king, behold, there came wise men from the east to Jerusalem, 2. Saying, Where is he that is born King of the Jews? for we have seen his star in the east, and are come to worship him.

Micah prophesied the birthplace of Jesus, and of the tribe from which he would come. It certainly came to pass. These prophets spoke from the mouth of the Lord and there could have been no doubt about them since these prophecies all came to pass.

What are we to learn from these prophecies?

1] When God speaks, it is final. We must believe the word of God. God will work in his time, not in our time.

2] The prophets foretold where Jesus would be born; that he would be scorned and rejected of men and it was so. We can take God at his word and wait upon him for its fulfilment.

3] Satan works at all times to spoil the plan of God for man, but if God tells us he is doing something, no plan of the devil can stop the Lord. When Herod set out to destroy the Christ child, he managed to kill all the little boys two years old and under. Unfortunately, there was a great cry in Ramah. Those poor mothers lost their young sons, but Jesus was not there. The Lord had ordered Joseph to flee with the young child and his mother into Egypt. God does not wait until a situation is in place before he works. He works ahead of the devil at all times. The Lord sees in the future and puts his plans into place before things happen, so that by the time things happen they have already been taken care of by the Lord.

4]   Jesus was prophesied to die the death of a criminal, but he was buried like a rich man, by a rich man in a new sepulchre. We can rest assured that so long as God has said it, it will end just as he has said.

5]   The prophecies of Christ's first coming were all fulfilled, despite the opposition of satan and his evil demons. God has ways and means of overthrowing whatever the devil would throw at us, in order that his word for our lives may be fulfilled.

6]   Jesus came in the fullness of time. *Galatians 4:4 But when the fullness of time was come, God sent forth his Son, made of a woman, made under the law.*
We may have to wait on the prophecy, but wait patiently, because in the fullness of time God will bring it to pass.

CHAPTER 6

OLD TESTAMENT PROPHECIES OF CHRIST'S SECOND COMING

What am I trying to do? I am trying to let my readers know that the prophecies of the First Coming of Christ were fulfilled perfectly, and the prophecies of his Second Coming will surely be fulfilled because the word of God is the truth. Here are a few Old Testament prophecies of Christ's Second Coming. We are looking forward to the fulfilment of all of these and must get ourselves ready to see them come to pass:

ISAIAH
Isaiah 65:17-19 *17. For behold, I create new heavens and a new earth; and the former shall not be remembered, nor come into mind. 18. But be ye glad and rejoice for ever in that which I create; for behold, I create Jerusalem a rejoicing, and her people a joy. 19. And I will rejoice in Jerusalem, and joy in my people: and the voice of weeping shall be no more heard in her, nor the voice of crying.*

Isaiah has seen in this prophetic message that God has created new heavens and a new earth for his people. The awful former things: sin and its consequence: sickness, famine, pestilence, drought, idolatry, witchcraft, murder, hate, envy, bitterness, sodomy, violence and crime, theft, and the like; shall not even be remembered. This will be a time of joy and happiness. There will be no more crying, no sorrow, no sighing because the former things will have passed away. What a day of rejoicing that will be? There is going to be peace for the people of God. The sacrifices we make to serve the Lord in this system will be fully repaid by the Lord. Our sufferings will all be over. May the Lord help us to live in accordance with the word of God so that we may be accounted worthy to enjoy these blessings that the Lord has prepared for those who love him.

DANIEL

Daniel 7:8-11, 18-22, 25-27 *8. I considered the horns, and behold, there came up among them another little horn, before whom there were three of the first horns plucked up by the roots; and, behold, in this horn were eyes like the eyes of a man, and a mouth speaking great things. 9. I beheld till the thrones were cast down, and the Ancient of days did sit, whose garment was white as snow, and the hair of his head like the pure wool: his throne was like the fiery flames, and his wheels as burning fire. 10. A fiery stream issued and came forth from before him: thousand thousands ministered unto him, and ten thousand times ten thousand stood before him: the judgment was set, and the books were opened. 11. I beheld then, because of the voice of the great words which the horn spake; I beheld even till the beast was slain, and his body destroyed, and given to the burning flame. 18. But the saints of the Most High shall take the kingdom, and possess the kingdom for ever, even for ever and ever. 19. Then I would know the truth of the fourth beast, which was diverse from all the others, exceeding dreadful, whose teeth were of iron, and his nails of brass; which devoured, brake in pieces, and stamped the residue with his feet; 20. And of the ten horns that were in his head, and of the other which came up, and before whom three fell; even of that horn that had eyes, and a mouth that spake very great things, whose look was more stout* *than his fellows. 21. I beheld, and the same horn made war with the saints, and prevailed against them; 22. Until the Ancient of days came, and judgment was given to the saints of the Most High; and the time came that the saints possessed the kingdom. 25. And he shall speak great words against the Most High, and shall wear out the saints of the Most High, and think to change times and laws, and they shall be given into his hand until a time and times and the dividing of time. 26. But the judgment shall sit, and they shall take away his dominion, to consume and to destroy it unto the end. 27.And the kingdom and dominion, and the greatness of the kingdom, shall be given to the people of the saints of the Most High, whose kingdom is an everlasting kingdom, and all dominions shall serve and obey him.*

We have a right to serve the God of heaven. Daniel saw and prophesied of the time of the end. Yes, Jesus is coming again. The thrones of the world rulers will be cast down and the Ancient of Days [our God] will sit on the judgment seat to do some judging. Daniel saw the greatness of our God. This makes me want to check up on myself just to ensure that I am serving this great God aright because it will be a fearful day for those who are not ready when he comes again. What seemed like fiery flame was proceeding from his all-powerful throne. His most righteous, white garment, was as the whiteness of snow, his hair like pure wool. A fiery stream seems to have issued forth from before him and he was ministered to by an innumerable amount of worshippers. The prophet Daniel was not able to count them. Daniel saw the destruction of the wicked one whose body was given to the burning flames.

The beast system is the wicked system of the world whose

reign opposes the commandments of the Lord. This system and all it stands for will be given to the flames. There is fire coming for all those who oppose God. These beasts represent world kingdoms which would arise but one would be worse than the others and that kingdom would rise up against the saints of the Most High. It would seem, according to Daniel's prophecy, that this kingdom would prevail against the saints and would think to change times and laws. All the devil's work, through man, would only be for a time, however, until the Ancient of days put an end to it and gives judgment to the saints, who in time, will possess the kingdom.

We have seen Daniel's prophecy in fulfilment in these last and final days of this age. There is a certain war against the saints. The rebellion of world leaders under satan's leadership have set out to wear out the saints as laws are framed to prevent the full promulgation of the truth of the gospel. God's people are under pressure of the world systems, as they work at almost forcing the Lord's people to comply with the sinfulness of the systems. God's true people will not bow even under severe persecution because they know that God will come to their rescue in due time. The enemies of the people of God will be thrown to the flames and the Lord's people will possess the kingdom. The kingdom which they will possess is an everlasting kingdom given to them by their king of Kings and Lord of lords and all dominions will serve and obey Him.

We are in the end of the age and Daniel has foretold what is now imminent. May the Lord help his people to be ready to meet him. Not only to be ready, but to work at evangelising the world for the Lord before he returns. **Daniel 12:3** *And they that be wise shall shine as the*

72

brightness of the firmament; and they that turn many to righteousness, as the stars for ever and ever. The children of God need to be wise in a wicked world that is hostile to the things of God. Wise people serve God. The wise shall shine in the kingdom of their father and for those of us who turn many to righteousness we shall be bright, and shine as the stars for ever and ever.

AMOS
Amos 4:11-12   11. I have overthrown some of you, as God overthrew Sodom and Gomorrah, and ye were as a firebrand plucked out of the burning: yet have ye not returned unto me, saith the Lord. 12. Therefore thus will I do unto thee, O Israel: and because I will do this unto thee, prepare to meet thy God, O Israel.

The church is spiritual Israel. The church knows all about how God overthrew Sodom and Gomorrah. It goes to say that sin brings down the fire of destruction and the church must walk right in the presence of the Lord. God has promised that unless people repent destruction like that of Sodom and Gomorrah is forthcoming. Man should therefore repent and turn to the Lord. The prophet warns: Prepare to meet thy God. The things that are happening today, the laws that govern the nations are many of them completely outside God's order and unless things change, nations are earmarked for imminent destruction. Jesus is coming soon and judgment is at hand. To escape the fires of hell, man must ask the Lord to save him, and confess the lordship of Christ. Again the word of God says: Prepare to meet thy God.

HABAKKUK
Habakkuk 2:14 For the earth shall be filled with the knowledge of the glory of the Lord, as the waters cover

the sea. When Jesus comes again the whole earth will be filled with the knowledge of God's glory. The darkness of this present age certainly obscures the glory of the Lord, but the time is coming when sin will be a thing of the past, and God's glory will be truly glorious. Praise the Lord.

ZECHARIAH

Zechariah 14:4-9 *4. And his feet shall stand in that day upon the mount of Olives, which is before Jerusalem on the east, and the mount of Olives shall cleave in the midst thereof toward the east and toward the west, and there shall be a very great valley; and half of the mountain shall remove toward the north, and half of it toward the south. 5. And ye shall flee to the valley of the mountains, for the valley of the mountains shall reach unto Azal; yea, ye shall flee, like as ye fled from before the earthquake in the days of Uzziah king of Judah: and the Lord my God shall come, and all the saints with thee. 6. And it shall come to pass in that day, that the light shall not be clear, nor dark: 7. But it shall be one day which shall be known to the Lord, not day, nor night, but it shall come to pass, that at evening time it shall be light. 8. And it shall be in that day, that living waters shall go out from Jerusalem; half of them toward the former sea, and half of them toward the hinder sea: in summer and in winter shall it be. 9. And the Lord shall be king over all the earth, in that day shall there be one Lord, and his name one.*

This is a very informative blessing prophesied by Zechariah. He tells us that the Lord our God shall come and all the saints with him. When Jesus came the first time he did not bring any saints with him, but at the second coming he shall come down from heaven with the saints. What an exalted position for the Lord's people. After we have borne the burden and heat of the day, we

74

shall enjoy the favour of our God. When Jesus came the first time, there was still night and day, but Zechariah has told us in his prophecy that there shall be no night in the new heavenly kingdom. There shall be no darkness. Praise the Lord. In the evening it shall be light. O yes, the Lord shall be king over all the earth. He came the first time to die for the sins of the human race. The prophet tells us that he is coming the second time to reign as King over all the earth. Come quickly Lord Jesus! The rulers of this present age are mere humans and they very often rule unjustly; multitudes everywhere are unhappy. However, our King Jesus shall set up his righteous kingdom and we shall have one Lord, and his name one. O how the Lord's people look forward to this glorious day, which we believe is fast approaching!

MALACHI

Malachi 4:1 *For, behold, the day cometh, that shall burn as an oven, and all the proud, yea, and all that do wickedly, shall be stubble: and the day that cometh shall burn them up, saith the Lord of hosts, that it shall leave them neither root nor branch.*

Malachi has seen the day coming which shall burn as an oven. Jesus is coming with fire and all the wicked ones shall be burnt up as stubble. Nothing will be left of them. When Jesus comes again, he is coming to judge the world in righteousness and all that do wickedly shall suffer the judgment of eternal fire. It makes sense to walk in the ways of the Lord. Many people live as though they have all the time in the world to make it right with God, but this is not the case; the signs of the time foretell that the end of all things is at hand. Sin is at an all-time high. Natural disasters have multiplied around the world. There are wars, famines, pestilences, unjust leaders in every area of society; the list is endless. All this tells of the fulfilment of prophecy and the imminent second coming of the Lord.

What can we learn from all this?

1]   That the prophets are men of God who are called by the Lord to foretell events. The prophecies of the first coming of the Lord all came to pass and we can trust these prophecies in like manner to come to pass in time.

2]   Isaiah has spoken of what we can expect in the new world order. This will be a time of joy and peace and only those who are prepared will enter into this holy system. We must therefore get ready to meet the Lord if we are to be a part of this glorious kingdom.

3]   The prophet Daniel has had revealed to him by the Lord the judgment to be meted out by the Lord when he comes again. He saw the greatness of the Lord, his authority and power. If the Lord's people hold out to the end, despite persecution, they will possess the kingdom. We should therefore expect difficult times, but should stand our ground to the end, because a crown of life awaits us if we do not faint.

4]   If we are wise, and evangelise and turn many souls to God's righteousness, we shall shine in the kingdom of the Lord.

5]   God's glory will fill the earth once sin has been completely dealt with and done away. Sin clouds over everything and often prevents man from beholding the glory of the Lord. However, when Jesus comes again, everything will be as God intended it to be and we should work at being a part of God's holy order.

6]   Seeing that the coming of the Lord is near, borne out by the things that are coming to pass, we should all prepare to meet our God. How do we prepare? We should walk in line with God's holy word. We should obey the commandments of the Lord as laid down in the holy scriptures.

7]   We have the assurance from prophecy and the sound word of God that our God shall be King over all the earth. All the worldly kingdoms shall pass away. They shall all be burned up and we shall be with Christ in a kingdom of peace, for ever.

MY FAITH TESTIMONY
by Pastor Rose

For many years I prayed for a breakthrough in my housing situation. I prayed and prayed and nothing happened. In my frustration, I said to the Lord, "Father, I don't understand why you are not answering my prayers. I know that you are perfect and that your word is true and you said in your word that you hear and answer ALL prayers. I know that this applies if we are within your will. Father, have I sinned against you? If I have Lord, has this sin stopped my prayer from being answered?" I had no reply for a long time, then one day the Lord gave me an answer through scripture – Habakkuk 2:3, which said, "For the vision is yet for the appointed time; It hastens toward the goal and it will not fail. Though it tarries, wait for it; For it will certainly come, it will not delay". I felt honoured and decided to wait to see what would happen next. About a year later, the Lord showed me a night vision. In it, he showed me a new property near to where I lived. He said that I would be offered this property but that although it was brand new and looked enticing, I should not take it but should wait a few days later and I would be offered another property. [In the vision, he took me to each property and showed me around them]. He said that I should take the second property. He then went into detail about where the property was, the colour of the front door, how many doors from the end of the road it was, the fact that it had a garden and that the garden could be seen from the end of the road through a side entrance. The vision was so detailed that I woke up feeling extremely confident. Two days later I was offered the first property. It was brand new and very tempting and looked exactly, in absolute detail, like the one in the vision, but I remembered what the Lord had said and turned the property down. Two days after that, I had another offer. This one was a house and was exactly like the one I was shown in the vision; it fit all the criteria. I took it immediately and moved in on the 15th July 2011.

The wait was long but it was all worth it. God sticks to his word. Sometimes we do not understand why the Lord takes a long time to answer our prayers but he said in his word, "though it tarries, wait for it". I waited and I am so glad I did. Sometimes what we are praying for is not yet ready; God has to make provision for our requests and put things in place so that those requests can come to pass.

If there is something you have been praying about for a long time and you have still not received it from the Lord, wait. God is assuredly working something out in your behalf. He will give you the best. He knows how to do it. He has to make the right thing available. He will not give you anything but the best. Learn to simply trust the Lord and he will give you the desires of your heart, in due time.

Strangely enough, God is able to do exceeding abundantly above all that we ask or think, according to the power that worketh in us.*[Ephesians 3:20].* God is faithful that promised.

Blessings.

CHAPTER 7

THE SIGNS OF THE TIMES FORETELL THAT OUR REDEMPTION DRAWETH NIGH

The Apostle Paul says, this: *1 Thessalonians 5:1-2 1. But of the times and the seasons, brethren, ye have no need that I write unto you. 2. For yourselves know perfectly that the day of the Lord so cometh as a thief in the night. 3. For when they say, Peace and safety; then sudden destruction cometh upon them, as travail upon a woman with child; and they shall not escape.*

No one needs to be told that there has to be a change in this system of things. The going is so tough and things are so terrible world-wide, there have been so many wars and natural disasters everywhere that Christians and non-Christians are aware that unless something happens for the better, mankind is heading for the destruction of himself.

I will endeavour to try and look at scripture with my readers and see where we are in time, what is happening and what will happen, and what we all should do to ensure we escape the things that are already coming upon us all.

Matthew 24:1-14, 21-25, 33-35, 40-44 1. And Jesus went out, and departed from the temple: and his disciples came to him for to shew him the buildings of the temple. 2. And Jesus said unto them, See ye not all these things? Verily I say unto you, There shall not be left here one stone upon another, that shall not be thrown down. 3. And as he sat upon the mount of Olives, the disciples came unto him privately, saying, Tell us, when shall these things be? And what shall be the sign of thy coming, and of the end of the world? 4. And Jesus answered and said unto them, Take heed that no man deceive you. 5. For many shall come in my name, saying, I am Christ; and shall deceive many. 6. And ye shall hear of wars and rumours of wars: see that ye be not troubled: for all these things must come to pass, but the end is not yet. 7. For nation shall rise against nation, and kingdom against kingdom: and there shall be famines, and pestilences, and earthquakes, in divers places. 8. All these are the beginning of sorrows. 9. Then shall they deliver you up to be afflicted, and shall kill you: and ye shall be hated of all nations for my name's sake. 10. And then shall many be offended and shall betray one another, and shall hate one another. 11. And many false prophets shall arise, and shall deceive many. 12. And because iniquity shall abound, the love of many shall wax cold. 13. But he that shall endure unto the end, the same shall be saved. 14. And this gospel of the kingdom shall be preached in all the world for a witness unto all nations; and then shall the end come. 21. For then shall be great tribulation, such as was not since the beginning of the world to this time, no, nor ever shall be. 22. And except those days should be shortened, there should no flesh be saved: but for the elect's sake those days shall be shortened. 23.Then if any man shall say unto you, Lo, here is Christ, or there; believe it not. 24. For there shall arise false Christs, and false prophets, and shall shew great signs and wonders; insomuch that, if it were possible, they shall deceive the very elect. 25. Behold, I have told you before. 33. So likewise ye, when ye shall see all these things, know that it is near, even at the doors. 34. Verily I say unto you, this generation shall not pass, till all these things be fulfilled.   35. Heaven and earth shall pass away, but my words shall not pass away.   40. Then shall two be in the field, the one shall be taken, and the other left.   41. Two women shall be grinding at the mill, the one shall be taken, and the other left.   42. Watch therefore; for ye know not what hour your Lord doth come.   43. But know this, that if the goodman of the house had known in what watch the thief would come, he would have watched, and would not have suffered his house to be broken up.   44. Therefore be ye also ready: for in such an hour as ye think not the Son of man cometh. **[Please read all of Matthew 24].**

I believe the disciples of Jesus felt good about their temple and they came to Jesus as he departed from the temple; to show him their beautiful buildings. King Solomon had set the trend for erecting beautiful temple buildings. However, Jesus was looking farther ahead and told them that everything of those buildings would be thrown down; would be destroyed. The disciples liked to ask questions of the Lord. They realised that he only knew the answers so they asked him privately the timing of those things and what would be the sign of his coming. They had heard Jesus speak of the fires of hell and of weeping and wailing and gnashing of teeth. They knew that Jesus would one day leave them and would be coming again and they needed to know what would lead up to his coming. Jesus took them through the whole story. It would be really great if people today would seek to know where we are in time. Let us look together at some of the signs of the time; you will need to fill in the ones I have left out yourself: this is to sharpen our understanding from scripture that we are in the end of the age: We should not allow ourselves to be deceived by anyone. Why? There would be false Christs and false prophets who would deceive many. There would be wars and rumours of wars, but we should not be troubled because all these things must come to pass before the end comes.

Nation would rise against nation, and kingdom against kingdom. There would be famines and pestilences and earthquakes in different places. Jesus said that this would be the beginning of sorrows. God's children would be hated and persecuted. Many would be offended and hate one another but those who endure to the end would be saved. There would be great tribulation such as had not been before and never will be again, and except the days were shortened by the Lord no one would be saved, but Jesus told the disciples that for the elect's sake he would shorten the days. Jesus warned his disciples of the deception that would take place. The disciples were told by the Lord not to listen to news that Christ was here or there because his appearance would be visible to all. They shall see the Son of Man coming in the clouds with power and great glory and he shall send his angels to sound the trumpet and gather his elect from the four corners of the earth. Jesus told them: When you see these things begin to take place, know that his coming is near.

Jesus gave a firm warning: *"Heaven and earth shall pass away but my words shall not pass away"*. He said that no man knows the day nor the hour when the Lord would come : the angels did not know; only the Father. It would be like this however: *As in the days of Noah people were eating and drinking, marrying and giving in marriage until that day when Noah entered into the ark and the floods came and took them all away.* Jesus said that people would be very busy, being unaware of the imminence of his return and he would come when they least expected him. There would be two people doing things together; one would be taken away and the other would be left. Why? One would be ready for his coming and the other would not be. Jesus told the disciples that the watchword is Watch, because no one knows when he is coming. They should be ready at all times because he said if the owner of the house knew that the thief would break in at a certain time he would watch and not allow his house to be broken into. His coming would be like a thief breaking into a home when the owner was not watching. Jesus, therefore, warned his disciples to be ready for his coming.

Jesus gave a parable about a wise and faithful servant whom his lord had made ruler over his house to take care of his household and feed them at the right time. There is a blessing for that servant if when his master comes he finds him doing what he was given to do. If, however, he thinks that his lord is delaying his coming and begins to ill-treat his fellow servants and lives carelessly, the lord is likely to come in a day when he does not expect him, and will appoint that unfaithful servant his portion with the hypocrites. There shall be weeping and gnashing of teeth.

What can we learn to help us from Matthew 24?

***Jesus detailed the signs of the times carefully to his disciples. Since Jesus Christ is the same yesterday, today and forever *[Hebrews 13:8]* we know that these teachings are for us. We should watch for the appearance of false Christs and false prophets and avoid them. We should not believe those who would point us to some alien Christ and tell us where to find him. Jesus' coming would be visible as the lightning comes out of the east and shines unto the west.

***Today, nation rising against nation is an ongoing problem. Wars are everywhere and rumours of wars. There are famines around the world. Our TVs and radios constantly seek help for the poor and needy in drought stricken areas. These are signs of the times foretelling of the Second Coming of the Lord.

***Earthquakes and tsunamis are a regular occurrence these days. We have watched on our TV screens the suffering from these great earthquakes around the world. The latest was the destruction of large areas of Japan from earthquakes and tsunamis. The news say that there are more earthquakes these days than the world has ever known. They seem to be one after the other. No one can do anything about this because it is pointing man to watch for the coming of the Lord.

***Iniquity is surely abounding. Sin is at an all-time high. The standard of morality is at its lowest ebb around the world and the so-called developed countries seem to be wallowing in the filth of sin, although they should know better. The word of God is put aside and satan and his demons seem to be having a field day. Sin is overflowing. Wrong is right and right is wrong in these last days. As the Lord's people we should take our stand for the righteousness of the Lord knowing that his appearance to judge the world is imminent.

***The gospel of the kingdom is being preached, despite the opposition of satan. False religions have found their way in many developed countries, but the gates of hell cannot prevail because the word of God is being preached via TV, radio and the internet. Missionaries are still taking out the truth that we are in the end of this world system, and the gospel of the kingdom is being preached, and the Lord's people must hasten with the word of God to rescue the lost. We must evangelise, now that we have such great means of doing so; [TV, radio, internet etc.]. I personally do a lot of teaching and ministry via the internet: by email and downloads. We will hasten the coming of the Lord if we will use the wide range of opportunities we have to turn the lost to the Lord. We must get out the gospel, because then shall the end come.

***Iniquity [sin] is overflowing and because of this the love of many is worse than cold. There does not seem to be much love in the world today. We must pray for governments and rulers of the world today: *1 Timothy 2:1-2 1. I exhort therefore that first of all, supplications, prayers, intercessions, and giving of thanks, be made for all men; 2. For kings, and for all that are in authority; that we may lead a quiet and peaceable life in all godliness and honesty. 3. For this is good and acceptable in the sight of God our Saviour.*

We need godliness in our societies if sin is to cease overflowing because love then becomes cold or non-existent. The murders, the thefts, the wars around the world, the violence and crime, the hate and bitterness and unforgiveness, [to name a few] is a sign of lack of love. If we love our neighbours we will not hurt them.

*** Talk about tribulation: Jesus said that it would be the worse type, such as was not since the beginning of the world, or ever shall be. Are we in this time? The trials and problems have multiplied over the last few years and most people today are stressed out. There are diseases that even the doctors cannot account for. The deadly diseases have multiplied over time because of the many chemicals we take into our bodies, by way of the food we eat and the medicines we take. Men, trying to help their fellowmen have ended up destroying them. Man is now lost and do not have the answer. The preaching of the gospel is the answer to all man's ills. God is willing and ready to help man if he will turn to him before it is too late.

***If we stay with the word of God we will not be deceived, being God's elect. The word of God is powerful enough to keep us, protect us and prepare us for the coming of the Lord. The Lord wants his children to spend time in his presence. That is what watching is all about. How can we spend time in his presence? By feeding upon the word of God and meditating it, and by praying always.

***When the Lord appears with the voice of the archangel, every eye shall behold him and all the tribes of the earth shall mourn. Why? Because they did not make themselves ready by obeying the word of God. The Lord's people shall not be like the unsaved who will mourn, but we shall meet our Lord with joy and gladness since we have been waiting for him.

***The signs we are seeing in these last days, obviously, point to the imminent return of the Lord to receive his people unto himself. The Lord Jesus told the disciples that when we see these things we should know that he is even at the doors.

***Jesus said, heaven and earth shall pass away but his words shall not pass away. These are very strong words coming from the Lord. He has told us that no man knows the day nor the hour when the Son of Man cometh; the angels do not know, only the Father, but we should remain faithful and watch.

*** We must not let the Noah's day overtake us. Many will be doing their own thing when the Lord comes. What should we do? We should live righteously and look forward to the coming of the Lord. We must prepare to meet our God; we must be ready. We must not be like the goodman of the house who is not watching and is allowing the thief to break into his house. We must not live carelessly and be unfaithful and let the Lord find us unprepared. We should be faithful and do what he has given us to do in righteousness and true holiness and he will reward us at his coming. The unfaithful servant will be cast out with the hypocrites, but the faithful servant will be blessed. We must live for the Lord so that we may be blessed of him at his coming.

Mark 13:20, 32-37 20. And except that the Lord had shortened those days, no flesh should be saved: but for the elect's sake, whom he hath chosen, he hath shortened the days. 32. But of that day and hour knoweth no man, no, not the angels which are in heaven, neither the Son, but the Father. 33. Take ye heed, watch and pray, for ye know not when the time is. 34. For the Son of man is as a man taking a journey, who left his house, and gave authority to his servants and to every man his work, and commanded the porter to watch. 35. Watch ye therefore: for ye know not when the master of the house cometh, at even, or at midnight, or at the cockcrowing, or in the morning. 36. Lest coming suddenly he find you sleeping. 37. And what I say unto you I say unto all, Watch.

Jesus went back to the Father after the resurrection and he is coming again to receive his saints unto himself, and we must wait for him. The word likens this waiting period to a man who has gone on a journey and has given various duties to his servants; he has also commanded the porter to watch. Again, the gospel of Mark commands us to watch as we do not know when our Lord is coming. The command to watch was not only for the disciples, it is also for us to day and we should heed the warning.

Luke 21:17-19, 25-28, 33-36 17. And ye shall be hated of all men for my name's sake. 18.But there shall not an hair of your head perish. 19. In your patience possess your souls. 25. And there shall be signs in the sun, and in the moon, and in the stars, and upon the earth distress of nations, with perplexity; the sea and the waves roaring; 26. Men's hearts failing them for fear, and for looking after those things which are coming on the earth, for the powers of heaven shall be shaken. 27. And then shall they see the Son of man coming in a cloud with power and great glory. 28. And when these things begin to come to pass, then look up and lift up your heads; for your redemption draweth nigh.

When do we need to look up and lift up our heads? When we see the things happening the way they are today. Why? Because our redemption is drawing near. Jesus is nearly here.

There has never been a time in the history of man that the whole world have the same problems. What is happening in the world today? The terrible shaking of the financial conditions; the confusion and fear of what is happening, is everywhere. Jesus said these signs will precede his coming and we should know that he is even at the door. He is coming in power and great glory; not the battered man on a cross, but King of kings and Lord of lords. May the Lord help us to be ready when he comes, in Jesus' name.

Acts 1:10-11 *10.And while they looked steadfastly towards heaven as he went up, behold, two men stood by them in white apparel: 11. Which said, Ye men of Galilee, why stand ye gazing up into heaven? This same Jesus, which is taken up from you into heaven, shall so come in like manner as ye have seen him go into heaven.*

The angels in this scripture reminds us today that as Jesus was seen going up into heaven, likewise he will be seen coming down from heaven to receive us unto himself. Just as the disciples looked up to see Jesus go, we will look up to see him come down. That is why Jesus admonished the disciples to, look up as they see scripture being fulfilled because he is on his way down.

What are we to learn from all these studies?

***That the scriptures are being fulfilled before our very eyes and we should be ready to look up to see our Lord coming down to receive us unto himself.

***Jesus, our master has left us work to do and we must be getting on with it; we must do the job he has given us to do properly, every one of us, because he will require it of us. Our job is to evangelise the world for Christ. We must live a holy life and get on with the charge of the Lord.

***Jesus has assured us that the things he has told the church about will definitely come to pass. He said, heaven and earth shall pass away, but his word shall not pass away. The word of God is dependable.

***The spirit of rebellion and disobedience is manifest in many so-called "first-world countries" where the bible was used as our rule of faith. In these last days leaders have caused the people to sin by passing laws contrary to scripture, but the Lord has told us that in our patience we should possess our souls. We must keep our souls alive in accordance with the word of God and not be moved, but rejoice because we know that the coming of the Lord is near.

***We must not allow the signs of the times to cause us to fear, but we should look forward to being with the Lord. We should look up. The Lord has promised to shorten the days for the elect's sake so please remember that all that is happening will not last.

CHAPTER 8

THE MIDNIGHT CRY

Most people in these last days are so busy that they cannot even hear their door bells ring. People, even Christians, are so stressed out by the wickedness of the system in which they live, that they find it hard to relax and study the word of God and pray, which is most essential if they are to hear the voice of God. However, they will hear the Midnight Cry which time is fast approaching. Listening to the Lord enables us to walk in righteousness and true holiness, without which no man shall see the Lord. *[Hebrews 12:14 Follow peace with all men, and holiness, without which no man shall see the Lord.*

Matthew 25:1-13, 31-46 [Please read all of it] 1.Then shall the kingdom of heaven be likened unto ten virgins, which took their lamps, and went forth to meet the bridegroom. 2. And five of them were wise, and five were foolish. 3. They that were foolish took their lamps, and took no oil with them: 4. But the wise took oil in their vessels with their lamps. 5. While the bridegroom tarried, they all slumbered and slept. 6. And at midnight there was a cry made, Behold, the bridegroom cometh, go ye out to meet him. 7. Then all those virgins arose, and trimmed their lamps. 8. And the foolish said unto the wise, Give us of your oil; for our lamps are gone out. 9. But the wise answered, saying, Not so; lest there be not enough for us and you: but go ye rather to them that sell, and buy for yourselves. 10. And while they went to buy, the bridegroom came; and they that were ready went in with him to the marriage: and the door was shut. 11. Afterward came also the other virgins, saying, Lord, Lord, open to us. 12. But he answered and said, Verily I say unto you, I know you not. 13. Watch therefore, for ye know neither the day nor the hour wherein the Son of man cometh. 31.When the Son of man shall come in his glory, and all the holy angels with him, then shall he sit upon the throne of his glory: 31. And before him shall be gathered all nations: and he shall separate them one from another, as a shepherd divideth his sheep from the goats: 33. And he shall set the sheep on his right hand, but the goats on on the left. 34. Then shall the King say unto them on his right hand, Come, ye blessed of my Father, inherit the kingdom prepared for you from the foundation of the world: 35. For I was an hungred, and ye gave me meat: I was thirsty, and ye gave me drink: I was a stranger, and ye took me in: 36. Naked, and ye clothed me: I was sick, and ye visited me: I was in prison, and ye came unto me. 37. Then shall the righteous answer him, saying, Lord, when saw we thee an hungred, and fed thee? Or thirsty, and gave thee drink? 38. When saw we thee a stranger, and took thee in? Or naked, and clothed thee? 39. Or when saw we thee sick, or in prison, and came unto thee? 40. And the King shall answer and say unto them, Verily I say unto you, Inasmuch as ye have done it unto one of the least of these my brethren, ye have done it unto me. 41. Then shall he say unto them on the left hand, Depart from me, ye cursed, into everlasting fire, prepared for the devil and his angels. 42. For I was an hungred, and ye gave me no meat: I was thirsty and ye gave me no drink: naked, and ye clothed me not: sick, and in prison, and ye visited me not. 44. Then shall they also answer him, saying, Lord, when saw we thee an hungred, or athirst, or a stranger, or naked, or sick, or in prison, and did not minister unto thee? 45. Then shall he answer them, saying, Verily I say unto you, Inasmuch as ye did it not to one of the least of these, ye did it not to me.

46. And these shall go away into everlasting punishment but the righteous into life eternal.

What a count down! I am going to try and go through this word of God with you, as to what it takes to enter into the Lord's kingdom at the end of the age, and at the end of our life on earth in this world system of things.

Everyone was busy doing his own thing in the world. There were some Christians who thought they loved the Lord with all their hearts, but the bible says they were divided into two groups. Jesus likened them to ten virgins [born again Christians]. However, five of them were wise and five of them were foolish. Both sets of virgins were on their way to meet the bridegroom. Jesus likened himself to a bridegroom and the church his bride. The church is on a journey to meet her bridegroom. Now the soul searching word here is that the church should be ready to meet her bridegroom. The bible says that there was a Midnight Cry: Behold the bridegroom cometh, go ye out to meet him. The foolish Christians were travelling at some point in their Christian journey without oil in their lamps. Obviously, they were saved, but somewhere along the way they lost the Holy Ghost [oil]; they quite possibly had allowed the cares of this life, the deceitfulness of the things of the world; the stresses and strains of life to dry them out; they had left off reading and meditating the word; had slackened up their attendance at church services and thus had become drained out. Does that ring a bell? The wise saints stood their ground in the face of persecution; distress, perils, temptations and the like and held on to their oil – the precious Holy Ghost who kept them safe and sound to meet their bridegroom. We need to remember that both virgins fell asleep while the bridegroom tarried.

Christians, let us keep our eyes open to what is taking place and know that the end of all things is at hand. Even the wise virgins fell asleep; became somewhat lethargic and half-dead, although they held onto their faith in the Lord.

How was the going with the foolish virgins? The word says they found out their mistake far too late. Quite frankly, it seems they thought they could straighten out their lives at the last minute; they left it unto the coming of the Lord. Wake up saints!! These poor souls began to seek to fill up with the anointing at the last minute. However, there was no time to get their lives right, so the bible says when they thought they were fit to enter the Lord's kingdom, the door was shut. The wise virgins held on to their faith and stayed in the word, even though at times they fell somewhat short. I believe when the wise virgins found they were falling asleep they went back to the word and to fasting and prayer. The bible says that when the foolish virgins came back after trying to "top up", the door was shut; the wise virgins had gone in with their bridegroom, safe and sound. The foolish ones knocked at the door, but it was too late. "Open unto us, open unto us", they cried, but the reply came back at them "I don't know who you are". There is a point of note here: When the foolish virgins found they were lacking in the requirements to enter the kingdom of heaven, at the last minute, they begged some help from the wise virgins. These were truly wise, because they told them to go and buy for themselves because they could not afford to leave themselves short of God's divine requirements. The ministers cannot help you when you are standing before the Lord; the righteous saints cannot help you. Get it right now before it is too late. Hear and obey the word as it is ministered unto you, while there is yet time. How often saints slacken up and take the word of God lightly!! That is what had happened in this parable that Jesus gave. They were going to church all right, but their hearts were not right with God. It is good to be called a virgin [a Christian]; it is better to live a Christian life and be ready to meet the Lord. Jesus gave the warning: *Watch therefore, for you know not the day nor the hour wherein the Son of man cometh.*

In the same chapter *[Matthew 25:14-30]*, Jesus gave another parable about the ten talents. A man was going on a far journey [Jesus went back to heaven after his first coming, and it seems to some that he has gone away for a long time]. He called his servants [the church] and gave them talents: He gave one five talents, to another he gave two talents and to another he gave one talent. The one who received five talents went away and put his talents to work and doubled them; the one who received two talents also went away and put his two talents to work and doubled them. The one who received one talent, hid his talent, and with an evil heart of unbelief called his master an austere man who wanted to reap where he had not sowed. Now, we have three types of servants of God. The first one with the five talents loved his master and was obedient to the word of God; he was a man with initiative and zeal and he used up and multiplied what the Lord had placed in him. So did the second. These were both commended by their Lord. *"Well done, good and faithful servant, thou hast been faithful over a few things, I will make thee ruler over many things. Enter into the joy of thy Lord. [Matthew 25:20-23].* These people received the blessings of the Lord. God could depend on them.

The one talent man would have received the same

blessings if he had used up his talent. Now, listen to this: It is Christ who works in us to do his good pleasure. Jesus would have blessed that man if he had doubled his one talent; he would have had two talents and had the same reward. What does this tell us Christian workers? We should not covet the people who seem to have more gifts or talents. God gives us gifts according to our abilities and he does not expect any more of us than our best. The one talent man did not think much of himself; he became jealous of the others and was not prepared to put his one talent to work. Result: He became corrupted in his mind to the point he blamed God and received unto himself total damnation from the Lord. His gift was taken away from him and given to the one who had the most, *and cast the unprofitable servant into outer darkness [hell]; there shall be weeping and gnashing of teeth- Matthew 25:30].* What a state to be in when Christians become slothful and unprofitable. May the Lord help us to put our talents to work and receive the rewards of heaven at his coming.

Judgment of the Nations: Jesus opened the scene of what it will be like at his coming. He explained that the Son of man shall come in his glory with his holy angels and he shall sit upon the throne of his glory. He shall gather before him all nations. Obviously, this would mean that wherever one is from: his culture, his race, his creed; he will have to appear before the Lord when he comes. No more time for repentance; this will be a time of reckoning. The sheep will be separated from the goats [the good from the bad]. The sheep will be placed on the Lord's right hand and the goats on his left hand. There is a lot of mixture of peoples in this system, but at the return of the Lord there will be a separation. On what side of the Lord will we be? On his right hand or on his left hand? Here we go! Then shall the King say to them on his right hand,

Come ye blessed of my Father, inherit the kingdom prepared for you from the foundation of the world. *[Matthew 25:34]*. Our destiny has been known by the Lord from the foundation of the world. That is why when we are being stubborn, the Lord sometimes chastise us to bring us to our senses, because he has a plan for our lives which he wants to bring into being. Some rebel and go their own way and others conform to the will of God. What is his will for our lives? That we repent and submit to his lordship in order that we may inherit eternal life.

I very often repeat *verses 35 -46 of Matthew 25*. Many of our Christian brothers and sisters often think that operating in the gifts of the Spirit, using up their many talents, e.g. singing, music, preaching, teaching, working of miracles, to name a few will get us into heaven. We sometimes deceive ourselves and overdo in the service of the Lord, thinking this will cause us to make it in; but Jesus has laid down what it takes to make heaven our home. We must watch ourselves to see whether we meet the criteria laid down in the Midnight Cry of Matthew 25. Here Jesus explained what it takes to measure up to God's standards to enter heaven. How we treat and minister to each other is most important: I was hungry and you fed me; I was thirsty and you gave me something to drink; I was naked and you clothed me; I was sick and in prison and you came unto me; I was a stranger and you took me in. We are sometimes so taken up with being busy in the hum-drum life of church work that we forget mercy and love for our brothers and sisters in the Lord, and to our neighbours [everyone]. Showing mercy and compassion is high up on God's list of priorities: visiting those who are sick and in prison and ministering to them both spiritual and practical help; feeding those who are unfortunate to be hungry and thirsty; giving some clothes to those naked ones; just exercising the love of God are basic essentials of making it in.

Jesus commended the righteous by telling them that they had fed him, clothed him, quenched his thirst, visited him when he was in prison and when he was ill [possibly in hospital], taking care of him whilst he was a stranger in some place. When the righteous asked when this had happened, he replied: *Verily I say unto you, Inasmuch as ye have done it unto one of the least of these my brethren, ye have done it unto me. [Matthew 25:40].* Keep helping somebody because you are doing it for the Lord and he will surely repay you when he shall sit upon his throne judging righteously. The righteous man was not being judged; he was facing the Lord to receive his reward. When we are saved the word of God judges us daily and corrects us and puts us in right standing with God. The unsaved man who has never repented of his sins and have never allowed the Lord to lead his life, must account to the Lord at the judgment.

If you are reading this and you are not saved, you can turn your life over to the Lord right now. Just ask the Lord to forgive you of your sins on the merits of his shed blood, and accept him as your Lord and Saviour. This is the best thing you will ever do in your life.

As for the man on the left hand of the King: I was hungry and you gave me no meat; I was thirsty and you gave me no drink; I was naked and you clothed me not; I was sick and in prison and you came not unto me; I was a stranger and you took me not in: The wicked man's answer: When did I see you in such a case and did not minister unto you? Reply: *Inasmuch as you did it not unto one of the least of*

*these my brethren, you did it not unto me. [**Matthew
25:41-45**].*

The Reward for the righteous: *Come ye blessed of my
Father, inherit the kingdom prepared for you from the
foundation of the world [**Matthew 25:34**].*

The Punishment for the wicked: *Depart from me, ye
cursed,into everlasting fire, prepared for the devil and his
angels. [**Matthew 25:41**]*

***Matthew 25:46:** And these shall go away into everlasting
punishment, but the righteous into life everlasting.*

What are we to learn from the Midnight Cry?

I will try and summarise what we are supposed to learn
from the Midnight Cry of ***Matthew 25.***

1] We are talking about the Coming of the Lord. Jesus
can come at any time, at a time we are least looking for
him. As the Lord's people we should be ready.

2] We should be careful not to be amongst the foolish
virgins; those Christians who tend to become lukewarm as
we await the coming of the Lord. It would seem that the
foolish virgins had not been watching and had lacked
study of the word, fasting and prayer; possibly also
neglecting fellowship with the believers in order to be
strengthened in their walk with the Lord.

3] It can be too late for us if we allow ourselves to fall
short of the Christian standard so that the Holy Spirit
draws away and leaves us empty and unable to face the

100

Lord at his coming.

4] There will not be time to get ready when the Lord comes. The foolish virgins went out to buy oil; to try and top up, but it was too late; the door was shut. This should be a warning to us all.

5] If we are watching and waiting for the coming of the Lord, we will prepare ourselves and his arrival will not come upon us as a surprise, because we will be expecting him. At the end of this parable Jesus warns the church: *Watch therefore, for ye know neither the day nor the hour wherein the Son of man cometh* [***Matthew 25:13***].

6] As regards the talents that the man travelling to a far country gave to his servants, we should see to it that we use up the gifts the Lord has given to us, for his glory. Two of the servants multiplied their talents by working them. The one with five talents gained another five; the one with two talents gained another two. These servants were commended by their Lord. He called them: *good and faithful servants*. We should work at receiving this kind of commendation from our Lord at his coming.

7] We should be careful not be like the one talent man who hid the Lord's gift. He was either covetous and lost the zeal to work his talent, since he was given only one talent; or he was just plain lazy and refused to have a good try at working what he was given. He blamed his lord, critized him and spoke evil words. His evil heart caused him to hide his talent and gave back only what he had received. His talent was taken away and given to the servant who had ten talents.

8] The man who had received the two talents and had

multiplied it by working it, was given the same commendation as the one who had worked five talents. We can only use what the Lord has given us and the one talent man would have received the same commendation as the other two if he had worked his one talent, and would have entered into the joy of his lord, like his fellow servants.

9] The slothful servant was sharply corrected by his lord and told he should have put his money in the bank where he would have earned interest. He was called "unprofitable" by his lord and banished into outer darkness where there is weeping and grinding of teeth. Beware church, don't get banished into outer darkness. Occupy until the Lord comes.

10] Jesus detailed what it takes to enter heaven in no uncertain terms. The King shall sit upon the throne of his glory in judgement. The righteous will not be judged but will be commended and given their reward of eternal life. *Come ye blessed of my Father, inherit the kingdom prepared for you from the foundation of the world. [Matthew 25:34].*

11] Jesus laid down the requirements to enter into the Lord's kingdom. These are our duties: love and compassion to our fellowmen. It is most important that we love our fellowmen and exercise kindness and mercy. We should be sure to visit the sick; feed the hungry; give something to drink to the thirsty [could be spiritual and natural]; clothe the naked; visit those in prison [could be spiritual and physical]; take care of the strangers – bring them into our homes and help them. We should not allow the wickedness of the world today, to prevent us taking people into our homes. Ask the Lord to show us those who are evil and would harm us if we took them in. *How God anointed Jesus of Nazareth with the Holy Ghost and with power, who went about doing good, and healing all who were oppressed of the devil, for God was with him. [Acts 10:38].* Jesus went about doing good, and so should we.

12] When we do good to others, as far as the Lord is concerned, we are doing it unto him. Jesus hurts when his children are suffering. We relieve our dear Lord of his suffering when we attend to the needs of others. It makes Jesus happy and for all that the Lord has gone through to pay for our salvation, we should do all we can to give him some pleasure.

13] There will be a separation of the righteous from the wicked when the Lord comes again. Be sure to be on the Lord's right hand. Those on the right hand of the Lord will hear *"Come"* and the ones on the left hand will hear, *"Depart"*.

14] When the Lord comes again, the wicked will all go into everlasting punishment and the righteous will enter into the joy of the Lord [heaven].

15] Hell was made for the devil and his angels, not for man and we should do all we can by obeying the word of the Lord to make heaven our eternal home.

My prayer is that all of us live for Jesus; walk in accordance with his word; love one another and prepare to meet our God so that the Midnight Cry does not come as a surprise to us, when it will be far too late for us to get ready. Jesus said we should be ready. *Matthew 24:44 Therefore be ye also ready, for in such an hour as ye think not the Son of man cometh.*

CHAPTER 9

CLEANING UP GOD'S CHURCH

Today, God's church seems to have fitted in nicely with the world. As Jude puts it: *For there are certain men crept in unawares, who were before of old ordained to this condemnation, ungodly men, turning the grace of our God into lasciviousness, and denying the only Lord God, and our Lord Jesus Christ. [Jude verse 4 –*Jude has only one chapter*].* Many strange teachings have found themselves into the church and much behaviour contrary to scripture is practiced. Sin does not seem to be too sinful in many places and in many cases, money seems to be preached instead of the gospel. God's holy altar has been broken down and many seem to be in the valley of decision and confusion, since they cannot find many of the teachings nowadays in scripture. Praise be to God, he will reserve himself prophets who have not bowed the knee to Baal neither have kissed him. *1 Kings 19:14,18 14. And he [Elijah] said, I have been very jealous for the Lord God of hosts: because the children of Israel have forsaken thy covenant, thrown down thine altars, and slain thy prophets with the sword: and I, even I only, am left: and they seek my life to take it away. 18. Yet I have left me seven thousand in Israel, all the knees which have not bowed unto Baal, and every mouth which hath not kissed him.*

Ephesians 4:1-3, 17-32 [read all of it] 1. I therefore, the prisoner of the Lord, beseech you that ye walk worthy of the vocation wherewith ye are called, 2. With all lowliness and meekness, with longsuffering, forbearing one another

104

in love. 3. Endeavouring to keep the unity of the Spirit, in the bond of peace. 17. This I say therefore, and testify in the Lord, that ye henceforth walk not as other Gentiles walk, in the vanity of their mind 18. Having the understanding darkened, being alienated from the life of God through the ignorance that is in them, because of the blindness of their heart: 19. Who being past feeling have given themselves over unto lasciviousness, to work all uncleanness with greediness. 20. But ye have not so learned Christ; 21. If so be that ye have heard him, and have been taught by him, as the truth is in Jesus. 22. That ye put off concerning the former conversation the old man, which is corrupt according to the deceitful lusts; 23. And be renewed in the spirit of your mind; 24. And that ye put on the new man, which after God is created in righteousness and true holiness. 25. Wherefore putting away lying, speak every man truth with his neighbour: for we are members one of another. 26. Be ye angry and sin not: let not the sun go down upon your wrath: 27. Neither give place to the devil. 28. Let him that stole steal no more: but rather let him labour, working with his hands the thing which is good, that he may have to give to him that needeth. 29. Let no corrupt communication proceed out of your mouth, but that which is good to the use of edifying, that it may minister grace unto the hearers. 30. And grieve not the holy Spirit of God, whereby ye are sealed unto the day of redemption. 31. Let all bitterness, and wrath, and anger, and clamour, and evil speaking, be put away from you, with all malice: 32. And be ye kind one to another, tenderhearted, forgiving one another, even as God for Christ's sake hath forgiven you.

What a word of cleansing from brother Paul. I think the church was in trouble in Ephesus. At the time Paul was ministering to these Gentile converts, they seemed to have found it difficult to turn completely from their former ways and it was taking the apostle a lot of teaching to straighten them out, and the rest of us! Paul begins by telling the church that serving the Lord was a vocation. Many of us who come to the Lord do not realise that this is a vocation; that we are a called out people who should shine forth for the Lord. Today, lowliness and meekness seem to be a thing of the past to most Christians. There seems to be an element of pride. Men crept in unawares are teaching that being blessed means the saints should be full of worldliness, forgetting that the church should not conform to the world. *[Romans 12:2 ...Be not conformed to this world, but be transformed by the renewing of your mind..]* Paul explained to the church then, and to us now that we should walk in the unity of the Spirit. No more disunity and pride amongst us, we need to come in the unity of the faith, because it is just one Lord, one faith and one baptism. The Lord does not want us to pull against each other as members of the Body, but stand together in unity to destroy the works of the devil.

When we are saved we are no more in the devil's kingdom, so we should not walk as the people of the world walk [those Gentiles, so to speak], we should walk as children of our Father in heaven. The understanding of the people of the world is darkened, they do not have the life of the Lord and their hearts are blinded by sin and satan. In the world, we were given over to uncleanness; we walked in the vanity of our minds, but the apostle Paul explained, in his cleaning up of the Ephesian church that we have not so learned Christ; the truth is in Jesus. The world lives a lie; the church must live the truth. I pray that the truth about purity will come back to the Lord's church. God's people in every age needs to put off the old man. The word of God is the same in every age. In

106

these last and evil days, many "crept in unawares" men are teaching that the church should cater for the new century. The word of God has already catered for every century. The church is admonished to put off her former way of life and walk in the newness of the Spirit of God. Our minds must be renewed and we should put on the new man which is created [or recreated] in righteousness and true holiness. Sometimes we are being asked to believe that there is another type of holiness than true holiness. Beware church, holiness is of God and the word of God is the holiness of God. The church must line up with the word of God. There are many lying spirits out today, seeking to deceive if it were possible, the very elect; it is not possible and God's true saints will continue to earnestly contend for the faith which was once delivered to the saints *[Jude verse 3]*.

Church, beware of anger and do not go to sleep with malice in your heart. Who knows whether one will wake up the next day! Should Christians steal? The bible says we should not steal. Pay those tithes and give those offerings; do not cheat in your time-keeping. May the Lord help us to check up on ourselves to see whether we are stealing. The apostle Paul was really doing a washing of the church with the word here, and may we give heed to these words. No sin can enter there!

What about corrupt communication and what is it? In the world it could be unclean words. In the church it could be those discouraging words to our Christian brothers and sisters when they endeavour to step out for the Lord. Those spiteful words which do not edify when the saints have excelled in their preaching, teaching or even their testimony. The word is advising us to look again at how we deal with each other. When we walk wantonly we grieve the Holy Spirit, and may the Lord help us to get our act right because we cannot go into heaven without the Holy Spirit; he has sealed us unto the day of our redemption. Besides, it is the Holy Spirit who shows us when we are going the wrong way.

I will stress *verse 31 of Ephesians 4.* The church of the Lord Jesus Christ should put away all bitterness, wrath, anger, boisterous behaviour, and all evil words from us and get rid of all malice.

How did the apostle sum up: Be kind to one another, tenderhearted, forgiving one another, even as God for Christ's sake has forgiven us. Unforgiveness is one of the worst sins. Why? If we do not forgive one another, our heavenly Father will not forgive us and we cannot go into heaven. *Matthew 6:15 But if ye forgive not men their trespasses, neither will your Father forgive your trespasses.* Did you see that? Did you hear that? Forgiveness is a must for the people of God. *Neither give place to the devil. [Ephesians 4:27].*

Romans 12:1-2, 9-21 1. I beseech you therefore brethren, by the mercies of God, that ye present your bodies a living sacrifice, holy, acceptable unto God, which is your reasonable service. 2. And be not conformed to this world: but be ye transformed by the renewing of your mind, that ye may prove what is that good, and acceptable, and perfect, will of God. 9. Let love be without dissimulation. Abhor that which is evil; cleave to that which is good. 10. Be kindly affectioned one to another with brotherly love; in honour preferring one another; 11. Not slothful in business; fervent in spirit; serving the Lord. 12. Rejoicing in hope, patient in tribulation; continuing instant in prayer; 13. Distributing to the necessity of saints; given to hospitality. 14. Bless them which persecute you; bless and curse not. 15. Rejoice with them that do rejoice, and weep with them that weep. 16. Be of the same mind one toward another. Mind not high things, but condescend to men of low estate. Be not wise in your own conceits. 17. Recompense to no man evil for evil. Provide things honest in the sight of all men. Dearly beloved, avenge not yourselves, but rather give place unto wrath: for it is written, Vengeance is mine; I will repay, saith the Lord. 20. Therefore if thine enemy hunger, feed him; If he thirst, give him drink: for in so doing thou shalt heap coals of fire on his head. 21. Be not overcome of evil, but overcome evil with good.

Here we go again about the cleaning up of God's church. The church needs to be clean to be caught up with the Lord in the clouds at his coming and so the Holy Spirit is giving us the instructions we need to get us ready for the coming of the Lord. In his writings to the Roman church the apostle Paul warns us about being conformed to the world. Resist the world's standards. These are contrary to the ways of the Lord. Try not to follow those Christians who think the Holy Spirit will always overlook some sin so long as they work for the Lord! There is a lot of that today. Holiness is the way into heaven. Without holiness no man shall see the Lord. *Hebrews 12:14 Follow peace with all men, and holiness, without which no man shall see the Lord.*

Our love for each other should be without pretence [dissimulation]. How we sometimes say things we do not really mean from the heart! How we pretend to like things we really do hate! How we bypass something we see our brothers and sisters do when we feel strongly about it! Stop pretending says the word of God. How

109

about being kindly affectioned? We are sometimes outright horrible to some of our brothers and sisters. The Lord loves the church and wants her clean and holy. Christianity does not give us leave to be lazy and slothful. God's people should occupy 'til he comes. Get busy in the Lord's business and operate your secular business with discretion. When those trying times come to us, may the Lord help us to continue in prayer; and be patient as we look to the Lord for our deliverance.

We know some saints who need to be distributed with some of our stuff: Food, shelter, clothing, a kind word, a visit whilst being ill, a visit to a relative in prison? What should we do? Get distributing! Is it easy to: *Bless them which persecute you: bless and curse not. [Romans 12:14]*. This is a hard saying, who can hear it? *John 6:60 Many therefore of his disciples, when they had heard this, said, This is an hard saying; Who can hear it?* Will you hear it? Yes we can hear it; yes, we have to hear it, if we are to make heaven our home. Where Jesus is, it's heaven. We have to bless those wicked people, even in our church who persecute us; who do us wrong. Jesus says we should not curse them. It is not easy but it is possible; in fact it has to be possible. We cannot do it in our strength. We can do it in the strength of the Lord if we will continue steadfastly in prayer, and we must render no man evil for evil. We cannot afford to retaliate because the Lord will not fight our battles if we do. We should do good to those who have hurt us and the Lord will bless us. Let God deal with our enemies. God will repay them. *Vengeance is mine saith the Lord, I will repay. [Romans 12:19]* To keep the church clean, we should let the Lord fight our battles. He knows how to fight them.

To try and fight life's battles in our own strength is to get things wrong. I love this word and often repeat it: *If thine*

110

enemy hunger, feed him; If he is thirsty give him drink; for in so doing thou shalt heap coals of fire on his head. [Romans 12:20].

When we do good to those who hate us, we get a release in our hearts and the joy of love will spring up in our hearts. About our enemy: He will be ashamed, become convicted of his evil ways to the point of a burning in his soul. It will be worse for him than if we had retaliated. And, you know what, he might repent and turn to God because of the love you have shown to him! What a wonderful church we would have; what a beautiful church, if we do not let evil overcome us but overcome evil with good. Do remember that we cannot observe these cleaning up admonitions in our own strength, but if we will trust the Lord and seek his help, we are more than able.

1 Corinthians 4:1-2 1. Let a man so account of us, as of the ministers of Christ, and stewards of the mysteries of God. 2. Moreover it is required in stewards, that a man be found faithful.

As the Lord's people we are stewards of his mysteries. God has revealed deep spiritual things to us and he expects us to be faithful to the trust. Everyone of us who receives Christ as our Lord and Saviour has been given gifts to enable us to do the will of God, for his glory, and we should not allow the devil and his cohorts to have anything to throw in the face of our precious Lord as to our unfaithfulness.

1 Corinthians 5:1-8 1. It is reported commonly that there is fornication among you, and such fornication as is not so much as named among the Gentiles, that one should have his father's wife. 2. And ye are puffed up, and have not rather mourned, that he that hath done this deed might be taken away from among you. 3. For I verily, as absent in body, but present in spirit, have judged already, as though I were present, concerning him that hath so done this deed. 4. In the name of our Lord Jesus Christ, when ye are gathered together, and my spirit, with the power of our Lord Jesus Christ, 5. To deliver such an one unto Satan for the destruction of the flesh, that the spirit may be saved in the day of the Lord Jesus. 6. Your glorying is not good. Know ye not that a little leaven leaveneth the whole lump? 7. Purge out therefore the old leaven, that ye may be a new lump, as ye are unleavened. For even Christ our Passover is sacrificed for us. 8. Therefore let us keep the feast, not with old leaven, neither with the leaven of malice and wickedness; but with the unleavened bread of sincerity and truth.

The apostle Paul had news that there was a type of fornication in the Corinthian church that was not even known amongst the Gentiles [the sinners] that a man should have his father's wife. Things have not changed. Today, many churches have forgotten that fornication is a sin. Many may not go as far as the Corinthian church, but it seems these days that people can cohabit and still be members of a church. These things ought not to be so and just like many "Christians" today those members seemed to have harboured sin instead of putting it away from them. Paul suggested that the fornicators be delivered to satan so that their carnal flesh could be destroyed. The old leaven [the old satanic nature] must be purged out of the church so that we may live a holy life. Christian leaders [like the apostle Paul] should see that the leaven of malice and wickedness be put away from the church in order that we may walk as new creatures in Christ. No

112

more fornication in the church brethren!! Heaven does not take in fornicators, adulterers or the sexually immoral.

1 Corinthians 6:9-11; 15-20   9. Know ye not that the unrighteous shall not inherit the kingdom of God? Be not deceived, neither fornicators, nor idolaters, nor adulterers, nor effeminate, nor abusers of themselves with mankind, 10. Nor thieves, nor covetous, nor drunkards, nor revilers, nor extortioners, shall inherit the kingdom of God. 11. And such were some of you: but ye are washed, but ye are sanctified, but ye are justified in the name of the Lord Jesus, and by the Spirit of our God. 15. Know ye not that your bodies are the members of Christ? Shall I then take the members of Christ, and make them the members of an harlot? God forbid. 16. What! Know ye not that he which is joined to an harlot is one body? For two, saith he, shall be one flesh. 17. But he that is joined unto the Lord is one spirit. 18. Flee fornication. Every sin that a man doeth is without the body; but he that committeth fornication sinneth against his own body. 19. What! Know ye not that your body is the temple of the Holy Ghost which is in you, which ye have of God, and ye are not your own? For ye are bought with a price: therefore glorify God in your body, and in your spirit, which are God's.

Here we go. What a clean up! The apostle Paul leaves none of the sexual immorality untouched. He digs at it at the very core. God wants his people in heaven, and we just cannot do what the unbelievers do. Out with sexual filth! The unrighteous shall not inherit the kingdom of God and of Christ. No adulterers, no fornicators, no effeminate [it seems this word is no longer in the world's dictionary; but it is still in God's good book], no idolaters shall enter God's holy kingdom. Let us get these sins out

113

of God's church. Those thieves who pose as God's people; those extortioners, those covetous people who want everything they see in the world's shops shall not inherit the kingdom of God and that is why the church must clean up her mess. Away with sin; away with the world, the flesh and the devil. Jesus is coming for a holy church, without spot and blameless. If the church does not know this: our bodies are the temple of the Holy Ghost which is in us [when we are living right], because we were bought with a price: with the precious blood of our Lord Jesus Christ. Church, we are not our own, Jesus bought us and we belong to him. We cannot, therefore, live as we like. Too much sin has crept into the church and God wants us to have a clean up to fit us for God's holy kingdom. Let us receive the word and allow it to clean us up. Each of us is a member of the church. Do, please remember that the sin of one of us can cause us to lose the battle, like it did when Achan sinned in the Israelite camp on their way to the promised land. *Joshua 7:1, 13   1. But the children of Israel committed a trespass in the accursed thing; for Achan, the son of Carmi, the son of Zabdi, the son of Zerah, of the tribe of Judah, took of the accursed thing: and the anger of the Lord was kindled against the children of Israel.   13. Up, sanctify the people, and say, Sanctify yourselves against tomorrow: for thus saith the Lord God of Israel, There is an accursed thing in the midst of thee, O Israel: thou canst not stand before thine enemies, until ye take away the accursed thing from among you. [read the whole chapter of Joshua 7].*

Sin in the church not only stops us going to heaven, not only prevents us from being ready for the Midnight Cry, here and now it causes us to lose the battles of this life. Why? God hates sin and will not be where it is, neither will he fight our battles until such time as we put away sin from the midst of us. Ministers, we must live holy and insist on holiness amongst the saints in order that we may fight the Lord's battles and win.

What can we learn from all this?
In Summary:

1] In accordance with *Ephesians chapter 4*, we should put on the new man and get rid of our former behaviour. We should give no place to the devil. Watch our speech. Our speech should be that which edifies and not speech which pulls down. Saints remember to live like Jesus: Be tenderhearted and forgiving, even as God in Christ has forgiven us. If we do not forgive one another, God will not forgive us and we will not go to heaven.

2] *Romans 12* instructs us how to keep clean for the Lord. We must not be conformed to the world's standards, but be transformed in the spirit of our minds. Our bodies must be presented as a living sacrifice, holy and acceptable unto God; and this is a reasonable service. It is definitely not unreasonable; it is for our own eternal benefit. Church, we should hate what is evil and cleave to what is good. Exercise brotherly love and remember to be patient in times of trouble, knowing that the Lord will bring us through. Here is a real challenge: Bless those who have done us wrong, yes, bless them, do not curse them, which is what the carnal mind was used to. Things are different now; we are saved; we are born again; our minds have been renewed by the Lord's Holy Spirit. And, how about taking care of our enemy? Feed him if he is hungry; give him something to drink if he is thirsty. Is this not what Jesus is doing for the world everyday? Is this not what he did on the cross for all of us? We should show forth the light of the Lord in this evil and sinful world. We will be rewarded by the Lord when he comes.

3]   The church has been made stewards of the mysteries of the Lord and the Lord requires that we be faithful to the charge he has committed unto us. We must give account at his coming; therefore, we cannot afford to be careless.

4]   The unrighteous shall not inherit the kingdom of God and of Christ. Sexual immorality is forbidden in the church of the Lord Jesus Christ and those who walk in this way shall not enter the Lord's kingdom.   Today, much sexual immorality is overlooked; the effeminate must not be so much as looked at; the same sex ones do not expect to be corrected and in some Christian environments this seems to be accepted behaviour. What is God's view on this? *Romans 1:26-27   26. For this cause God gave them up unto vile affections: for even their women did change the natural use into that which is against nature: 27. And likewise also the men, leaving the natural use of the woman, burned in their lust one toward another; men with men working that which is unseemly, and receiving in themselves that recompence of their error which was meet.*   God's view of this is that he has called it: vile affections and he says in *Romans 1:32* that those who commit such things are worthy of death. It sometimes get said that God is love and takes no delight in hurting people. God is truly love and that is why he does not want his children to walk in sin and receive eternal damnation.

Bottom Line: Get the filthiness out of the holy place; keep the house of the Lord clean and **Prepare to meet thy God.** *[Amos 4:12].*

MY TESTIMONY OF ANOTHER
GREAT MIRACLE FROM THE LORD
By Apostle Dr Daisy Lake

I have so many testimonies of the miracle working power of our great and all-powerful heavenly Father, who cares for us and looks after us in every condition of life.

My youngest daughter lives in Birmingham and I used to go up to see her every week and spend a day or two, just to see them. She had had her first child and he was six weeks old. I went up as usual but during this time I was sometimes spending the weekend to help her with the new baby, and to be there for her. God knows all things and he was watching the situation. I stayed with my daughter that weekend and planned to return to London the Wednesday evening in order to be home to attend our Thursday evening service.

It was winter and on this particular Wednesday it was very icy; there was some snow, and the roads were very icy. Her husband had been away on mission work away in Africa, and she was alone in the home with the baby when I was not there. I had my bags packed and she had telephoned for a minicab to take me to the station to get the train back to London on that Wednesday evening. As I was about to leave her, she looked at me and said, "Mummy I am going to London with you, I don't want to stay here on my own". I believe she was feeling a bit lost and lonely, since her husband was away and I was about to leave. "I will drive down to London with you", she said. "The road is very icy Mum, so I think we had better go in the morning". We cancelled the minicab and I settled down again. I was in the habit, as I still am, of going to bed rather late. That evening I got out the ironing and began to help her with it. I ironed until quite late; it was probably about 2.30am when I packed up and went into the bathroom. Karen [my young daughter] was downstairs watching the TV. She had left the baby sleeping in the cot. Where I was doing the ironing was very near to the room in which baby Timothy was sleeping. When I went into the bathroom Timmy was still sleeping. However, Karen must have heard the sound of the baby whilst she was downstairs. I did not hear him because I was in the bath. What I did hear, though, was a frantic knock at the bathroom door. "Mummy, Mummy, Timothy cannot breathe. Open the door, Open the door". I got out of the bath as fast as I could with no clothes on. I grabbed hold of the baby who was by this time almost breathless. He was struggling to catch his breath. I threw him up in the air, in the hope that he would be shaken into breathing. That is what we mothers do when our babies are choking. This did not seem to work and he was getting worse. I realised that satan and his demons were at work and I began to plead the blood of Jesus. "The blood of Jesus, the blood of Jesus, the blood of Jesus" I shouted. I quickly dragged on a long frock which I normally wear indoors and I was barefooted. On my head was the head gear I had on in the bath. In the icy car, with the iced up windscreen we sped down the road to the nearest hospital. I had the baby in my arms and I prayed and prayed and prayed. I shouted with authority, "The blood of Jesus, the blood of Jesus, the blood of Jesus". I bound the demons that had my daughter's first son and my beautiful baby grandson in bondage. I shouted out, "Get out of him, you demons, in the mighty name of Jesus; Loose him and let him go, satan; he belongs to Jesus; go back to the pit of hell, you devil, in the mighty name of Jesus". I fought for Timothy. This was a battle indeed. When we got to the hospital, my daughter asked for a doctor as quickly as

118

possible. Strangely enough the receptionist began to ask questions, "What is his name? What is wrong?" I spoke out, "The baby is very poorly and cannot breathe, please get a doctor". I continued to plead the blood of Jesus and to authoritatively command the demons to go. By the time the doctor had come, the baby sneezed five times and brightened up. He was delivered. Jesus had come to our refuge. The demons had been bound and God's warring angels had fought them off. Praise the Lord.

Why did I plead the blood of Jesus? The Lord had revealed to me the power that goes forth against the devil and his demons when we plead the blood of Jesus. The blood of Jesus is one of the most powerful tools the Lord has given to the church to combat the forces of darkness, anytime, anywhere and everywhere. When we plead the blood of Jesus we can never lose a battle against the enemy; the blood of Jesus reminds the devil and his cohorts that the price to deliver man from his evil works, has been paid and he is being told, and forced, to release his victims. It reminds the devil that man has been bought back to God by the blood of Jesus and he has to throw down his weapons of lies and deceit and flee. When we say, "the blood of Jesus, the blood of Jesus, the blood of Jesus", it puts God's warring angels to work on our behalf, since they can feel the power of the blood of Jesus, and hear the name of Jesus, which moves them to rise up quickly to our cries for help. These angels are ministering spirits who minister for us who are heirs of salvation. *Hebrews 1:14: Are they not all ministering spirits [the angels] who minister for us who shall be heirs of salvation.* When we call upon the all powerful name of Jesus all heaven bows and things begin to happen; heaven sees Calvary's cross and rushes to our aid. The authority and power in the sound of the name of Jesus cause those demons to tremble! tremble! tremble! When we say, "the blood of Jesus," the blood of Jesus and the name of Jesus come into force. The name of Jesus is revered in heaven, in earth and in hell; everything quakes at the sound of that great name. The victory is ours as we put these weapons of our spiritual warfare to work; use them. I did; I always do, and I have good success and victory in every condition of life. This is how it's done: Plead the blood of Jesus as many times as necessary and do not stop until you get the victory. Satan and demons must give in. Shout the name of Jesus in like manner and again don't stop until you get the victory. Jesus has given the church authority to walk all over the enemy, and nothing shall by any means hurt us. You should request and read my books : *The Blood of Jesus Revealed* and *The Wonderful Name of Jesus.*

The doctors did the usual tests on Timmy, after that spiritual battle, and there was nothing to find. However, they asked us to remain in the hospital with the baby for the rest of the night. I stayed in the room with baby Timmy and continued to pray. In the morning they discharged us.

My daughter went home and fetched some clothes for me. We travelled down to London later in the morning. Thank God for Jesus.

God sees everything before it happens. The Lord would have me to stay in Birmingham that night. He had my daughter wishing to travel down to London with me. Had she not have asked me to stay because the Lord had put it into her heart to come home with me, she would have been left alone with the baby in the house. There would have been no one to help her in the middle of the night because all the neighbours would have been asleep and she would not have been able to leave the baby to call anybody to help her. There would have been no one to hold the baby for her so she could drive down to the hospital. Only God knows what would have happened, but the Lord did not allow it to happen. To Jesus be all the praise and glory. O how I love Jesus! This is something I will never forget, and I have never forgotten. Jesus is precious.

A point of Note: Evangelist Blake, one of our ministers, saw into the spirit realm that very night. He saw multitudes of demons standing around my daughter's house. He alerted his wife Veronica. Wake up and let us pray; and he prayed. He told me this as I related to him what had happened. Thank God for praying saints. That is why God's people should always stand together. We have battles to fight and we have to watch for each other. Those demons had come that night to steal and to kill and to destroy, but Jesus had come into the world and payed the price for us, that we might have life and have it more abundantly *[St John 10:10]*.

God sees all things and had this case worked out before it came to pass. He is faithful that promised. He would not allow me to mourn, nor my young daughter. Our Timmy is growing up into a bright and lovely child who loves our blessed Lord, who has fought for him and kept him alive; who has delivered him out of the hands of satan and his evil demons. Praise the Lord. Dear reader, if you have not yet submitted your life to the Lord Jesus, please do so now. You never know what will happen and when. Thank God, both myself and my daughter were living for the Lord and still are. If we did not know Jesus we would not have known how to pray and what to do to drive away the demons. God saved us out of the hand of the enemy. The bible says that *whosoever shall call upon the name of the Lord shall be saved.* ***[Romans 10:13].*** That night we were saved from the wickedness of the devil. Do not leave it any longer, if you are not saved, ask Jesus into your heart. Ask the Lord to take away your sins. "Lord be merciful unto me, a sinner". Cry out: "Lord save me from sin and satan, in the name of the Lord Jesus". Call upon the name of the Lord. Say, "Jesus, save me, please save me". You have called upon his name; you have asked Jesus to save you and you must believe that he has saved you, and you can be assured that you have been saved. This puts you in a position of security and it gives you authority to discharge the evil demons from your life. It is a very honourable position. Not only so, God will send angels to help you in your time of greatest need.

Lots of love and blessings.

CHAPTER 10

HOW DOES THE CHURCH OVERCOME?

In order for the church of Jesus Christ to overcome all that is coming upon the earth in these times of stress and strain: of natural disasters; of mass unemployment whilst world governments are working towards the so-called New World Order; of mass apostasy; of an all-time high level of immorality; of sexual degradation of the basest sort; of sodomy and gross idolatry worldwide; of corruption in high places; of oppression of the poor and the like [the list is far too long for me to continue]; the church must take the word of God seriously as never before. There are certain sections of the Christian community who do not even believe some of the scripture. May the Lord help them; we are in the end of the age and the church must overcome all these things that are coming upon the earth, if she is to enter into eternal life. It is not a time to guess at the word of God; it is a time to take God at his word and walk in accordance with it.

Ephesians 6:10-18 10. Finally, my brethren, be strong in the Lord, and in the power of his might. 11. Put on the whole armour of God, that ye may be able to stand against the wiles of the devil. 12. For we wrestle not against flesh and blood, but against principalities, against powers, against the rulers of the darkness of this world, against spiritual wickedness in high places. 13. Wherefore, take unto you the whole armour of God, that ye may be able to withstand in the evil day, and having done all to stand. 14. Stand therefore, having your loins girt about with truth, and having on the breastplate of righteousness; 15. And your feet shod with the preparation of the gospel of peace; 16. Above all, taking the shield of faith, wherewith ye shall be able to quench all the fiery darts of the wicked. 17. And take the helmet of salvation, and the sword of the Spirit, which is the word of God; 18. Praying always with all prayer and supplication in the Spirit, and watching thereunto with all perseverance and supplication for all saints.

In order for the church to be ready at the coming of the Lord she must be prepared. How does she do this? The Lord's church must put on the whole armour of God which the apostle Paul outlines in the above scripture. I will attempt with you to try and break this down so we can understand how we allow this scripture to work for us and help prepare us for the coming of the Lord.

Verse 10: *Finally, my brethren, be strong in the Lord and in the power of his might:* It seems Paul was giving some final instructions to the church, some instructions of utmost importance. How are we to be strong in the Lord? The Lord is his word. We can only be strong in the Lord if we allow the word of God to dwell in us richly in all wisdom. *[Colossians 3:16a].* We should feed on the word of God day and night, take in as much of it as possible on a daily basis and allow the word to work in our lives. We should be wise as to obedience to the word. The word will show us when we have done wrong and give us the answer to correct our mistakes; it will keep us measured day by day to bring us up to the measure and stature of Christ. ***Psalm 119:105*** *Thy word is a lamp unto my feet and a light unto my path.* If we set our hearts on obeying the word of God it will become a lamp to our feet and it will bring light to the way we walk. The bible says *[Matthew 4:16] The people that sat in darkness saw great light, and to them which sat in the regions and shadow of death light is sprung up.* Jesus, the word of God, has brought light to a dark world to a people who were in the shadow of death. Man was doomed to die but the Light of the world came and brightened man's path. We must, therefore, each day, ensure that we are wearing the word of God, which is able to make us wise unto salvation. As we get the word inside us it will remove all sin and take away all weight which so easily ensnares us and it will enable us to run with patience the race that is set before us. Looking unto Jesus the Author and Finisher of our faith. Therefore, first and foremost, we must be clothed with the word of God. Jesus taught us these famous soul-searching words: *St John 6:63 It is the Spirit that quickeneth; the flesh profiteth nothing; the words that I speak unto you, they are spirit and they are life.* To be ready when the Lord comes, we must get rid of the carnal nature because it does not profit, it will eat away at our souls, but the Spirit gives life, and the word of God is spirit and life. Be immersed in the word of God and *Prepare to meet thy God. [Amos 4:12].*

Verse 11: Put on the whole armour of God , that ye may be able to stand against the wiles of the devil. We need to have on day by day the whole armour of God, if we are to stand against the wiles of the devil. Satan is crafty and deceitful and seeks ways and means to draw the Lord's people away by his lies. We must beware. Satan tempted Jesus, the Son of God, and said, "Command these stones to be made into bread", and get eating. He knew he was talking to Jesus but he still tried it on. He somehow thought he could trick the Son of God into obeying him.

Jesus used the word against the devil. To remain committed Christians we must be ready at all times to push back the powers of darkness as they come out against us, by standing our ground on the word of God.

Satan's wiles [tricks] vary from disease germs [cursed disease germs, which he calls sickness]; covetousness [which he calls ambition]; idolatry [which he calls religion]; sodomy [which he calls sexual preference]; hate/bitterness/retaliation [which he calls justice, because he says they deserve being hated and hurt in return for what they have done]; and the list goes on - all contrary to the ways of God.

We cannot lose a battle, if we know who is fighting them for us. We are well able to overcome the wiles of the devil, in whatever shape or form they come.

Verse 12: *For we wrestle not against flesh and blood, but against principalities, against powers, against the rulers of the darkness of this world, against spiritual wickedness in high places.* Paul was instructing the church. We are not fighting against people. Let us get it right; the devil is behind all our mishaps. He works through people. It is not your brother, it is not your sister, it is not your employer, it is not the neighbour; call it the right name, it is the devil and his cohorts. They work hard at using man to destroy man and to make us all miserable, but we must know who is behind our problems and use the weapons God has given to the church to fight those demons off. The evil laws that are pushed on us and which are corrupting our children and the nation, are what the enemy has planned in hell. Hell is the dark regions and satan and his demons have set out to keep people in bondage in the darkness of hell. The princes of this world work in high places. They aim for where there is control and authority over nations; this way they can reach more people to destroy them. However, we must be assured that the princes of this world come to nothing *1 Corinthians 2:6 Howbeit we speak wisdom among them that are perfect: yet not the wisdom of this world, nor of the princes of the world, that come to nought.* Did you hear that? The princes of this evil world come to nothing. Stand your ground against them, Jesus has brought them to nothing by the shedding of his precious blood, and we must cripple their works by the power of the blood of Jesus Christ. We have the victory over all these evil principalities. They tend to try to rule over whole nations at a time, but all we need is the word of God to reach these nations and this will bring their evil works to nothing and free up the people to serve our wonderful Lord Jesus.

When you are about to become angry at people and things, remember who you should be angry with and with whom you should do battle. It is the devil and the fallen princes of darkness. The light of the Lord in us will bring them to nothing and spoil their works.

Verse 13: Wherefore take unto you the whole armour of God, that ye may be able to withstand in the evil day and having done all to stand. We are admonished by the apostle Paul to take unto us the whole armour of God; not a part of it, but the whole of it. Often we are willing to wear only some of the armour. We enjoy putting on the lighter armour, but when it comes to the heavier ones; the ones that seem to ask for too much dedication; too much commitment; too much faithfulness; some of us tend to draw back. No, we must be prepared to take unto us the whole armour of God. Any exposed area leaves us open to the attack of the devil. Satan is always looking for an opening into which he can enter our lives to destroy what God has made us to become. Cover up saints, cover up completely. It is only in this way that we will be able to withstand in the evil day; the day when the devil is striking hard at us. When we are completely covered up with the full armour we are strong because the Holy Spirit will help us as we walk in obedience to the word of God, and angels will come to our aid. There will be no place where the devil can strike. His fiery darts will bounce back at him from off the covering of righteousness with which we are clothed.

Verse 14: *Stand therefore, having your loins girt about with truth, and having on the breastplate of righteousness. What is truth?* Pilate asked, *[St John 18:38].* The word answers this: **St John 14:6** *Jesus saith unto him, I am the way, the truth, and the life: no man cometh unto the Father, but by me.* There you are, Jesus is the truth. We must be girded up at our loins, which needs to be kept firm, with Jesus, and our chest must be covered with the breastplate of holy living. How often we get it wrong and expect the Lord to work for us. We cannot do what is wrong; we cannot walk sinfully and expect the Lord to fight our battles for us. Jesus will fight our battles when we walk in the light; when we walk in accordance with the word of God. Satan can work in darkness; he is confused when the light is shining and runs for cover. Demons are blinded by the light of the word of God in us, much more so when we are walking in line with it. We must not allow the devil to touch our hearts, we will die spiritually. We must not allow him to stab at our hearts spiritually, and this he will do if our hearts are covered with sin. However, satan and his demons lose the battle

128

every time when we are covered with the righteousness of God. The devil is always trying to unclothe us by tempting us to sin. We must not fall for his evil devices.

Verse 15: *And your feet shod with the preparation of the gospel of peace.* Where are we going? We should be travelling on those feet with the gospel of the kingdom. O how we walked to the places where the devil walked whilst we were under his control! Thank God, all that is over now and we can take the peace of God to those who are sick and suffering; those who are confused; those who are stressed out; those who are unhappy and can see no way out. Tell them this great news: *Jeremiah 29:11* *For I know the thought that I think toward you, saith the Lord, thoughts of peace and not of evil, to give you an expected end [a future and a hope].* Before we were shod with the preparation of the gospel [the good news] of peace, we told our friends and family, our relatives and neighbours about what the system can do for us, what the medical profession can do for us, what the different workers in the system can do for us; which did not give them peace but only more confusion. Now with the good news of the peace of God which passeth all understanding, their hearts and minds can be filled with the love of God. Joy and happiness then comes where sadness once had been.

Verse 16: *Above all, taking the shield of faith, wherewith ye shall be able to quench all the fiery darts of the wicked.* I love this verse. I do love all the rest of the verses, but this one does something special for me. **Shield** defined: A piece of defensive armour carried in the hand or on the arm to protect the body from blows or missiles. Do you know how harmful missiles can be if one is not protected from them? Satan and his demons are daily hurling his

129

evil missiles at people for the sole purpose of killing them. The reason we need the gospel is because it teaches us how to stop these attacks by the devil. We must hold onto our shield and get it in the right place to protect us from harm. The bible says we shall then quench the fiery darts of the wicked one. Those darts he fires are meant to burn us down to the ground and we must defend ourselves with our shield of faith. **What is faith?** *Hebrews 1:1 Faith is the substance of things hoped for, the evidence of things not seen.* Faith says we are strong, confident and determined and that when we stand upon the word of God and use it against the lies of the devil, we have won. Faith says we cannot lose a battle because the Lord is the One who fights our battles. *2 Chronicles 20:15 And he said, Hearken ye, all Judah, and ye inhabitants of Jerusalem, and thou king Jehoshaphat, thus saith the Lord unto you, Be not afraid nor dismayed by reason of this great multitude; for the battle is not yours, but God's.* Did you hear that? King Jehoshaphat was up against his wicked enemies, but the message came that they should not be afraid, because God would fight the battle for them. In these last days, we do need to stand by faith and let God fight our battles. When we walk in faith and let God fight, we cannot lose a battle. If we fight in our strength we will lose, and if we continue to lose battles we will fall and will not be ready at the coming of the Lord.

Verse 17: And take the helmet of salvation, and the sword of the Spirit, which is the word of God. We have to see to it that our head is covered. Where does one wear the helmet? On the head of course. It is our spiritual headgear, our spiritual covering for our minds. If our head is bruised we will become weak, so we have to see to it that our minds are stayed on God. Satan would like to bruise our heads and turn us silly!! We must cover our heads with our salvation, which is our security in God and our confidence in Jesus that he will take care of us, because we are his children. We must always walk in the knowledge that we are children of the Most High God, that the devil is under our feet and we have been given authority by Jesus to tread on the devils works and keep them under our feet. *Luke 10:19 Behold I give unto you power to tread on serpents and scorpions, and over all the power of the enemy: and nothing shall by any means hurt you.* We must keep this word of God in our hearts and minds at all times to enable us to get to work and walk over the devils plots and plans, knowing that he cannot hurt us. The word of God is all powerful to overthrow satan and his evil devices. Begin to speak the word in the face of the devil and his demons. Tell him what Jesus has said, and let him know that we believe it and are walking in it. Praise the Lord. We will not allow satan and his cohorts to destroy our salvation by his lies and deception. We have power over him. Use this power and take victory in the mighty name of Jesus.

Verse 18: *Praying always with all prayer and supplication in the Spirit, and watching thereunto with all perseverance and supplication for all saints.* Prayer is a must, but we are admonished to pray always with all prayer. We should pray about everything if we are to save ourselves from the devil's wiles. Prayer builds us up and moves mountains. Prayer is allowing God to take hold of our situation and allowing him to work it out for us. Prayer is putting God in control. Prayer gets us watching. Jesus says, *What I say unto you, I say unto all, Watch [Mark 13:37].* We must pray in the Spirit of the Lord; we must pray the word of God. We must use scripture in our prayers and take God at his word. Jesus told his disciples to watch and pray. *Matthew 26:41: Watch and pray that*

131

ye enter not into temptation.... If we do not watch and pray we will enter into temptation. Satan will tempt us to the uttermost, and we will not have the strength to overcome if we do not watch with the word and prayer. As we pray the Lord will minister to us how we should live, what we should do and not do and show us the way to go day by day. We cannot afford to slacken our watchfulness and our prayers. God wants us to persevere in prayer for all the saints. Thank God for the prayers of the saints. I do not know how I would manage without the prayers of the Lord's people and we should all pray one for another. *The effectual fervent prayer of a righteous man availeth much. [James 5:16].*

These verses of scripture [spiritual tools] are to protect us; they are to enable us to fight for our spiritual lives and get us ready for the imminent return of the Lord. May the Lord help us to live in the Spirit of the Lord as we go on from day to day.

In Summary

1] Whilst living in the kingdom of the Lord, in order to maintain our stand as Christians, we should ensure we put on the whole armour of God, and keep it on.

2] Satan and his demons will come out against us and we must be aware that we are at war at all times. We should therefore be ready to fight.

3] We cannot fight spiritual battles with carnal weapons, because our struggle is not with flesh and blood, but against principalities [princes of darkness], against powers, against the rulers of the darkness of this world. We therefore need our spiritual weapons to wage war against wicked spirit beings.

4]   We should stand by faith and know that we have been given authority by the Lord Jesus to demonstrate power over the power of the enemy and nothing shall by any means hurt us. The works of the devil will never be able to harm us if we stand upon the word of God.

5]   The sword of the Spirit, the word of God, is God's all powerful weapon to combat the works of darkness and we should be ready with it, in our hearts, and in our mouths, at all times. Why in our mouths? Because we should speak out loud the word of God. Satan knows that the word is the truth and he has to bow at the sound of God's holy word.

6]   Prayer should be a way of life for the Lord's people, since by prayer we place situations in the hands of God. Remember, the battle is not ours, it is the Lords, once we give it to him.

7]   We should always remember to pray for our Christian brothers and sisters that God will deliver them as we persevere in prayer for them.

8]   Minister the good news to others since this will give them peace. The world does not have peace but the gospel will give it peace and we should get the gospel out.

9]   Keep on your armour, resist the devil, walk by faith and let Jesus fight your battles, and heaven will be your home.

MY TESTIMONY OF DELIVERANCE
By Sister S

I was told that I had cancer of the breast.

Psalm 103:3 *Who forgiveth all thine iniquities; who healeth all thy diseases.*

It was on a Wednesday evening in February 2006 when I came in from work, as usual, and sat on my bed smoking. My right breast did not feel right, somehow, and I began rubbing it. To my surprise I felt a lump in the breast. Needless to say, I was quite shocked at this and said, O my God, this is it now! I rang my three sons and told them the bad news. I also rang my mother in the United States of America and told her what was happening in my body. She was, to say the least, as sad as I was. You must get down on your knees and pray, she told me. I took what she said on board and started to pray. The following day I went to see my doctor and told him what I had found in my breast. He immediately came over to me and felt the lump. He advised the receptionist to ring the hospital and make an appointment for me to see a specialist. This was done, and I went off to the hospital in due time, where they did all the necessary tests. Result: I had cancer of the breast. I prayed morning, noon and night, asking the Lord for his help. I was worried. The doctors told me to attend the hospital for the necessary therapy. I started to attend.

Jesus knows how to bring us out of our suffering, for his glory. A friend came to my house, in my time of darkness, and told me that there was a church in Stockwell where miracles were taking place. Because my need for healing was so great, I decided to attend. When I got to this house of prayer, I could feel the presence of the Lord. As the service went on, the invitation was given for those with special needs to come to the altar for prayer. I went forward. Apostle Lake brought me through the repentance and confession prayers so that I may receive the salvation of the Lord. After this, she prayed for my needs. She cursed the cancer and decreed my healing with a verse of scripture from *Isaiah 53:5 But he was wounded for our transgression, he was bruised for our iniquity, the chastisement of our peace was upon him, and with his stripes we are healed.* The Christian workers gave me some study material, and sold me a copy of Apostle Lake's book: *The Blood of Jesus Revealed.*

As soon as I arrived home from the meeting, I started to read the book and began pleading the blood of Jesus. As I read the book, and pleaded the blood of Jesus, I felt like someone was squeezing my body like a piece of cloth, and that things were being drained out of my body. God had taken the cancer out of my body. I went to church and testified of the miracle working power of God. I felt well. I went back to the hospital for a further check-up. There was no sign of the cancer. God had completely healed me. Thank you Jesus.

Following on, one night not long after my healing, I went to bed and dreamt seeing a well, in which I jumped. I woke up the next morning wondering what this could mean, after all what was I doing in a well; I cannot swim. I went back to church where I gave my testimony about the well. One of my Christian brothers told me to read the gospel of St John. As I read, the Lord spoke to me: I needed to get baptized in water. I was baptized at the next baptismal service. I completely surrendered my life to the Lord, and with his help I will never look back. Satan had set out to kill me, but my heavenly Father had rescued me. I now look forward to the services and I am enjoying the sweetness of God.

Jesus is precious. Whatever your need, pray; however bad your situation, plead the blood of Jesus; shout out the name of Jesus; hold on to the power of the Holy Spirit; and stand your ground in faith. Jesus will deliver you. He has delivered me and he will deliver you because he loves you. There is nothing too hard for the Lord.

Psalm 30:2 *O Lord my God, I cried unto thee, and thou hast healed me.*

CHAPTER 11

WHO GIVES US THE POWER TO OVERCOME?

JESUS, JESUS, JESUS.

St John 15:5 *I am the vine, ye are the branches. He that abideth in me, and I in him, the same bringeth forth much fruit, for without me ye can do nothing.* Isn't this quite clear? Jesus says, and rightly so, that without him we can do nothing. All the power belongs to God. He made us and knows our every need; he knows all about us. We were never made to operate without the Lord and since he is the vine and we are the branches, then the branches cannot live without the vine. Jesus Christ is our hope and stay. We are all helpless and weak without him and we cannot ever hope to overcome the works of the powers of darkness without Jesus. Since all power is in the hands of the Lord, then the power of the devil must submit to the higher power. The power the devil has is what God has allowed him to have and it is in Christ that we can exercise God's power.

Philippians 2:6-13 *6. Who, being in the form of God, thought it not robbery to be equal with God: 7. But made himself of no reputation, and took upon him the form of a servant, and was made in the likeness of men: 8. And being found in fashion as a man, he humbled himself, and became obedient unto death, even the death of the cross. 9. Wherefore God also hath highly exalted him, and given him a name which is above every name: 10. That at the name of Jesus every knee should bow, of things in heaven, and things in earth, and things under the earth; 11. And that every tongue should confess that Jesus Christ is Lord, to the glory of God the Father. 12. Wherefore, my beloved, as ye have always obeyed, not as in my presence only, but now much more in my absence, work out your own salvation with fear and trembling. 13. For it is God which worketh in you both to will and to do of his good pleasure.*

Jesus says: *He that* overcometh, *the same shall be clothed in white raiment; and I will not blot out his name out of the book of life, but will confess his name before my Father and before his angels.[Rev.3:5].* We have to overcome the things that are coming upon the earth if we are to make it into God's heavenly kingdom when Jesus comes, but we cannot do it in our own strength. Who is going to help us! The church has a captain of her salvation called the Lord Jesus Christ and this is what the bible says of him: This Jesus made himself of no reputation and took on sinful flesh to condemn sin in the flesh. He came as a servant in the likeness of men and became obedient unto death, even the death of the cross. I love this wonderful verse **[Philippians 2:9]** which lets everyone know [and that includes the devil] that God hath highly exalted Jesus after he had gone to the cross to die for humankind, and given him a name that is above every name. The name Jesus is the highest and most famous in the entire universe. Makes me glad to know that we have such a One to defend us and fight our battles for us. At this great name **JESUS** every knee, yes, also every demon knee, shall bow, of things in heaven, of things in earth, and of things under the earth [satan and his evil hosts] and every tongue [also satan's tongue] shall confess that Jesus Christ is Lord to the glory of God the Father. That makes us secure under the leadership of our Jesus. We shall overcome as he fights off our evil foes and enables us to live a victorious Christian life, fitting for eternal life.

Luke 10:18-19 18. And he said unto them, I beheld satan as lightening fall from heaven. 19. Behold, I give unto you power to tread on serpents and scorpions, and over all the power of the enemy: and nothing shall by any means hurt you.

If we meditate upon these powerful words of Jesus, we will overcome because we will know who has given them to us. Satan was thrown out of heaven and Jesus saw his fall; he came down as fast as a lightening flash. He was kicked out with speed. Jesus then gave the church power to keep satan and his demons, these serpents and scorpions who know how to sting; under our feet. It is the power that Jesus has given to the church that enables her to tread upon our enemies and in doing this, they are forbidden by the word to hurt us. What victory the church has been given by Jesus! May the Lord help us to rise up and begin to exercise the power the Lord has given us, over the power of the devil and his evil demons. We will never overcome unless we walk upon these evil, wicked, fallen beings who were thrown out of heaven. Satan and his demons have been in heaven, they know the blessings that await the people of God, and they are going all out to prevent us entering into the inheritance the Lord Jesus has provided for us. We must overcome them in the mighty name of Jesus!

These fallen beings are a snare to the human race, but the Lord has given us power over their evil works, to overcome them and rescue souls from the fires of hell. Let us rise up and do it in Jesus' name.

Matthew 16:18-19 *18. And I say also unto thee, That thou art Peter, and upon this rock I will build my church; and the gates of hell shall not prevail against it. 19. And I will give unto thee the keys of the kingdom of heaven: and whatsoever thou shalt bind on earth shall be bound in heaven; and whatsoever thou shalt loose on earth shall be loosed in heaven.*

There you are, Jesus has built the church upon the revelation of the word of God [Jesus himself] and the gates of hell shall never prevail against God's holy church. The enemy does try hard to bring the church down. He has always been unsuccessful because the word of God is the truth. The church has always won and will continue to win every battle through Jesus Christ our Lord. The church will forever overcome by the power of the word of God. At the cross Jesus secured the spiritual keys to deliver us, obtained by the shedding of his blood. The price had been paid, the battle won, Jesus became victor over the dark domain and handed the spiritual keys over to the church. With these spiritual keys we are commanded to bind and loose: bind the works of the devil, and loose the inhabitants of the world from their bondage to sin and satan, and free them up to serve the Lord and inherit eternal life. When we do some binding here on earth, it is confirmed in heaven; likewise when we loose here on earth, it is confirmed in heaven. Why? Jesus' blood has been placed at the highest position before the Father in heaven. The blood of Jesus is in the Royal Courts of Justice in heaven. Heaven says, Yes to our binding and loosing because of the shed blood of Jesus. The bible says: *Psalm 119:89* *For ever, O Lord, thy word is settled in heaven.* Through the blood of Jesus Christ we are overcomers.

Matthew 18:18-20 *18. Verily I say unto you, Whatsoever ye shall bind on earth shall be bound in heaven; and whatsoever ye shall loose on earth shall be loosed in heaven. 19. Again I say unto you, That if two of you shall agree on earth as touching any thing that they shall ask, it shall be done for them of my Father which is in heaven. 20. For where two or three are gathered together in my name, there am I in the midst of them.*

The bible says that in the mouth of two or three witnesses a matter is established *[2 Corinthians 13:1; Deuteronomy 19:15],* and if two of us shall agree on earth as touching any thing that we shall ask, it shall be done for us of our Father which is in heaven. That is why I call my prayer partners day by day and pray over difficult situations. United prayer is powerful and the word said that we will have what we ask the Lord for. We overcome as we unite in prayer and as we agree on matters pertaining to our well-being and that of others. Unity is strength, and united we stand. If we stand alone and fall there will be no one to pick us up, but if we walk in unity and we fall someone will lift us up.

Revelation 1:16-18 *16. And he [Jesus] had in his right hand seven stars: and out of his mouth went a sharp twoedged sword: and his countenance was as the sun shineth in his strength. 17. And when I saw him, I fell at his feet as dead. And he laid his right hand upon me, saying unto me, Fear not; I am the first and the last: behold I am he that liveth, and was dead; and behold, I am alive for evermore, Amen, and have the keys of hell and of death.*

What are the seven stars in the right hand of the Lord? These are the ministers of the seven churches who are at the place of the Lord's given power to rule over the works of the devil. The word of God coming from the mouth of Jesus [the sharp two-edged sword] is for cutting down the evil works of darkness. Speak the word of God against your problems and see them disappear! Jesus' countenance was shining because of his holiness. It was so bright! The apostle John fell at the feet of the Lord. In today's language we would say that "he passed out". The brightness and holiness of the Lord was too powerful for him to be able to stand up. Jesus had brought a message of great hope: Fear not; I am the first and the last. There is none before Jesus and there is none after him. John [and the church] was reminded that it was the same Jesus who had died for the sins of the world, but that he is alive for evermore. Thank God for that. Jesus is alive to keep us alive. Jesus has the keys of hell and of death. Since Jesus has overcome, we are now overcomers in his name. Hell and death have been defeated and we say Amen to that; praise the Lord.

The trek up Golgotha's hill was all worth it. *"Jesus paid it all; all to him I owe; sin had left a crimson stain; he washed it white as snow"* and I say Amen to these couple lines of song. Death no longer has dominion over us and we must work at reaching the lost for Christ so that they too will be overcomers through Jesus Christ our Lord.

When you are backed up against the wall and can see no way out to victory, shout out the name JESUS, JESUS, JESUS. This great and all powerful name says: "Victory is mine." We are overcomers through faith in his name.

What can we learn from this?

1] Jesus has given the church the power to overcome.

Why? At the name of Jesus every knee shall bow, of things in heaven, and things in earth, and things under the earth; And every tongue shall confess that Jesus Christ is Lord, to the glory of God the Father. Every thing and everybody, including satan and his cohorts must bow to the name of Jesus and we are overcomers in his name.

2] Jesus has given the church power over all the power of the enemy. We should take hold of the authority given the church by Jesus, and use the authority. We must command satan and his demons to release his captives. They must loose their hold because Jesus paid the price for man's liberation. Satan and his demons know this; our legal right has been secured by the blood of Jesus and they must set those captives free.

3] Use the blood of Jesus and the name of Jesus over every condition of life and see God at work. Heaven and hell responds at the sound of the blood of Jesus and at the shout of the name of Jesus. The sword of the spirit proceeding out of the mouth of Jesus is his word. When we speak the word of God, Jesus is the power behind it and demons must flee. Stand upon the word of God and be overcomers, in the mighty name of Jesus.

4] What we bind on earth is bound in heaven, and what we loose on earth is loosed in heaven. Begin to bind and loose. Bind the powers of darkness in the lives of believers and unbelievers. Demons antagonise believers and deceive unbelievers. These evil spirits must loose their hold because when we minister, it is confirmed in heaven and the victory is ours. Don't be afraid, go ahead and begin to exercise the authority the Lord has given us; the victory is ours, in the mighty name of Jesus.

5] Now for agreement prayers: When the going is tough, Get your prayer partner and begin to pray the word of God. God will listen to his word and perform it. Speak the word together, pray together and see the difference. Agreement prayer is powerful. Speaking the word in agreement is most powerful to bring the power down. See the rain of blessings fall and souls released from the bondage of satan; see your problems solved through unity and togetherness, in the name of Jesus.

6]   Jesus has the keys of hell and of death. The devil no longer has dominion over the church of God. His lying power has been taken away through Calvary's cross. Jesus went down into hell and whipped the devil and his demons in their very territory. He took the keys of hell and of death from the devil and set the captives free. We are free today, and we shall know the truth and the truth shall make us free, and whom the Son shall make free, shall be free indeed. *[St John 8: 32, 36].* We are free, praise the Lord.

MY TESTIMONY
By Sister E

The Blood of Jesus is very much alive

Towards the end of the year 2006, my husband and I decided to take a trip to Jamaica to visit our relatives and friends. Before we left, Pastor Lake and all the ministers prayed for us, and asked God to protect us and keep us safe.

The island was absolutely beautiful, the weather was lovely and the people very friendly. One day we went on

144

a long journey. On our way we stopped and prayed and the cab driver was very blessed. On our way back, I realized that my husband was very upset, but I took it very lightly. We got home ad went to bed. At about 1.30am I heard my husband calling me, to say that he was not feeling well. I jumped up and switched on the light. My husband looked lifeless and his eyes were bulging out of his head. I became very frightened and confused, so I poured out a cup of hot water from a flask and tried to feed him. He did not respond. I thought of calling my niece to get a cab to take him to the hospital, as there was no other form of emergency service.

Suddenly, I remembered a miracle I had witnessed at church, when a young girl collapsed on the floor, and was clinically dead. As a Registered Nurse with thirty years experience, I checked her out at the time and there seemed to have been no form of life, so I called the ambulance, which took over fifteen minutes to arrive. As I was preparing to resuscitate the little girl, I saw the ministers stoop over her; they were pleading the blood of Jesus in a very forceful way. She opened her eyes and started breathing. By the time the ambulance arrived, the child was up and walking, so there was nothing for them to do.

Suddenly, my faith became strong and I started to plead the blood of Jesus over my husband, and I found myself screaming to Jesus for help. I was then taken away: I could not hear myself screaming anymore, neither could I see nor feel my husband. When I came round, I saw my husband sitting at the edge of the bed drinking the cup of hot water. I shouted out these words: "You are alive; Thank you Jesus, you are my Shepherd".

God delivered us again. The ministry of the blood of Jesus

really works. My God is faithful, and I also thank Apostle Lake and all the ministers and saints who prayed, not only for our outgoing, but for our incoming.

There are some tough times in our lives when it seems there is no one around. Always remember, Jesus has promised, he will never leave us nor forsake us. *[Hebrews 13:5]*. Whatever need you may have, Jesus will meet it; whatever difficulty you are facing, Jesus will bring you out. Our God is faithful.

God bless you.

CHAPTER 12

THE LORD JESUS COMES DOWN FROM HEAVEN FOR HIS CHURCH

It is going to be a glorious day when Jesus comes again. With all that is happening in these last and trying days: the cashless society; the high standard of immorality and lawlessness; the hopelessness of the human race around the world; the sin of idolatry being magnified alongside the sin of witchcraft; the spirit of sodomy; the persecution of the Lord's people in more ways than one and the spirit of anti-Christ staring us in the face, it is high time to look up and lift up our heads, because our redemption draweth nigh. *Luke 22:28 And when these things begin to come to pass, then look up, and lift up your heads; for your redemption draweth nigh.* It is time to ensure that we are ready to meet the Lord and to work at having our spiritual garments white.

1 Thessalonians 4:13-17 13. But I would not have you to be ignorant brethren, concerning them which are asleep, that ye sorrow not, even as others which have no hope. 14. For if we believe that Jesus died and rose again, even so them also which sleep in Jesus will God bring with him. 15. For this we say unto you by the word of the Lord, that we which are alive and remain unto the coming of the Lord shall not prevent them which are asleep. 16. For the Lord himself shall descend from heaven with a shout, with the voice of the archangel, and with the trump of God: and the dead in Christ shall rise first: 17. Then we which are alive and remain shall be caught up together with them in the clouds, to meet the Lord in the

147

air: and so shall we ever be with the Lord.

Time is turning into eternity; the people of God are awaiting with eagerness the blessed appearing of our Lord Jesus Christ. We anticipate this great day. The songwriter says: And O my Lord prepare my soul for that great day. O wash me in thy precious blood and take my sins away. Yes, we have to be prepared and be ready as we wait. It is not a time to be pursuing worldly things; it is not a time to seek after silver and gold, albeit there is nothing wrong with these; it is a time to pursue righteousness because without holiness, no man shall see the Lord. *Hebrews 12:14 Follow peace with all men, and holiness, without which no man shall see the Lord.*

Looking at *verse 13 of 1 Thessalonians 4* it seems some of the saints were very sorrowful at the death of their loved ones, and the apostle Paul took time to encourage them and to explain to them the blessedness awaiting those who die in the Lord. What a great day that is going to be! I feel so excited as I write. Jesus is definitely going to keep his promise to his saints that he will come again and receive us unto himself. The word says that the Lord himself shall descend from heaven with a shout, with the trumpet call of God. Jesus will not be sending someone for us; he will be coming himself, and it does not stop there, he is going to bring those who sleep in Jesus with him. God is so faithful and fair in all his ways: those who have died will rise from the dead first; those who are still alive will be caught up together with them to meet the Lord in the air, and listen to this: So shall we ever be with the Lord. We are going to be with the Lord for ever. We shall see him with our very eyes. Praise the Lord! O happy day! Come quickly Lord Jesus. *[Revelation 22:20].*

148

1 Corinthians 15:19-26, 50-58 [read through the whole chapter]. *19. If in this life only we have hope in Christ, we are of all men most miserable. 20. But now is Christ risen from the dead, and become the firstfruits of them that slept. 21. For since by man came death, by man came also the resurrection of the dead. 22. For as in Adam all die, even so in Christ shall all be made alive. 23. But every man in his own order: Christ the firstfruits; afterward they that are Christ's at his coming. 24. Then cometh the end, when he shall have delivered up the kingdom to God, even the Father; when he shall have put down all rule, and all authority and power. 25. For he must reign, till he hath put all enemies under his feet. 26. The last enemy that shall be destroyed is death. 50. Now this I say, brethren, that flesh and blood cannot inherit the kingdom of God; neither doth corruption inherit incorruption. 51. Behold, I shew you a mystery; We shall not all sleep, but we shall all be changed. 52. In a moment, in the twinkling of an eye, at the last trump: for the trumpet shall sound, and the dead shall be raised incorruptible, and we shall be changed. 53. For this corruptible must put on incorruption, and this mortal must put on immortality. 54. So when this corruptible shall have put on incorruption, and this mortal shall have put on immortality, then shall be brought to pass the saying that is written, Death is swallowed up in victory. 55. O death, where is thy sting? O grave, where is thy victory? 56. The sting of death is sin; and the strength of sin is the law. 57. But thanks be to God, which giveth us the victory through our Lord Jesus Christ. 58. Therefore, my beloved brethren, be ye stedfast, unmovable, always abounding in the work of the Lord, forasmuch as ye know that your labour is not in vain in the Lord.*

This is a scripture that I have used at funerals. I love to preach it; it is so wonderful. What a hope for the believer!

149

Thank God it is not in this life only we have hope and my prayer is that the whole human race will find hope outside this present life. This life is full of troubles; that is why man needs the after life which Jesus Christ offers. Paul explains to the saints that Christ is the firstfruits of those who died, the first to come back from death, as an example of the resurrection from the dead of the believer. The first man [Adam] brought death into the world. The second man [Jesus] brought the resurrection of the dead. One plunged the human race into the darkness of death; the other pulled the human race out of the darkness of death into the light of life. I love this: *Then cometh the end*. Saints, stop worrying about all that is taking place in this life. The end is coming; all our wicked enemies shall be under the feet of our Lord; and death, the last and worst enemy shall be destroyed.

How do we enter God's holy heavenly kingdom? The apostle Paul explains this to the church. At the appearing of our Lord, we shall be changed. Flesh and blood cannot inherit the kingdom of God. This corruptible body shall not enter God's kingdom but we shall be changed. In the twinkling of an eye, at the last trumpet; the trumpet shall sound and the dead in Christ shall be raised incorruptible and we shall be changed. This perishable body shall put on an imperishable body and this mortal shall put on immortality and at this point death shall be swallowed up in victory. No more sting of death; no more grave to hold our bodies down; complete freedom and victory at last!! Praise the Lord. Who has given us this great victory? JESUS CHRIST our Lord. Now for one of my favourite verses in scripture, the verse I often use to encourage the brethren at home and abroad to continue in the work of the Lord, knowing that their labour is not in vain, in the Lord. I encourage them with this verse to be steadfast in the faith and keep going on with the Lord, despite the trials of this life. *1 Corinthians 15:58 Therefore, my beloved brethren, be ye steadfast, unmovable, always abounding in the work of the Lord, forasmuch as ye know that your labour is not in vain in the Lord.*

1 Corinthians 2:9-10 9. But as it is written, Eye hath not seen, nor ear heard, neither have entered into the heart of man, the things which God hath prepared for them that love him. 10. But God hath revealed them unto us by his Spirit: for the Spirit searcheth all things, yea, the deep things of God.

The scripture has declared in many places how wonderful it will be for the children of God at the coming of the Lord, but it tells us here that although we may sometimes try to imagine the glory of the Lord that the saints will enjoy, try as we may it is unimaginable. In this earthly and low state the bible says that it has never entered into our hearts the wonders of what God has prepared for those of us who love him. Let us just love the Lord with all that is within us, bless his holy name and do our best in his service. I often tell the Lord that my best is just not good enough, but I can't do more. Jesus is so wonderful, he deserves our best. Lord, we give ourselves to you completely; help us to do our best at all times as we anticipate your imminent return.

In Summary:
1] Jesus is coming again to receive his people and to reward their faithfulness.

2] When the Lord returns his archangel will give the

trumpet call and the dead in Christ shall rise first. God is faithful, he will first bring up those who have gone through the sting of death. Those of us who are alive at his return will be caught up together with them in the clouds to meet the Lord in the air.

3] At the trumpet call, in the twinkling of an eye, very quickly, we shall be changed. We will put on a body which cannot decay but will continue forever; a glorious body and we shall be like our Lord.

4] We have hope of a better life because if it was in this life alone we had hope we would be most miserable. This life is full of troubles and difficulties with death at the end; thank God, however, our hope is in the life hereafter, where there will be joy and peace for ever. A glorious place that the Lord has gone to prepare for us. *St John 14:1-3 1. Let not your heart be troubled: ye believe in God, believe also in me 2. In my Father's house are many mansions: if it were not so, I would have told you. I go to prepare a place for you. 3. And if I go and prepare a place for you, I will come again, and receive you unto myself; that where I am, there ye may be also.* When Jesus comes again, he has promised to take us to that place he has prepared for us. We are a prepared people for a prepared place.

5] Death will be a thing of the past. The sting of death is sin. Sin will be no more and so death will be no more. Death has a way of separating us from our loved ones. All that will be in a past forgotten, praise the Lord! Death will be swallowed in victory.

6] We have the victory, through Jesus Christ our Lord. God is faithful and he will bring it all to pass. We should, therefore, be steadfast, unmovable, always abounding in the work of the Lord, forasmuch we know that our labour is not in vain in the Lord.

7] We shall surely be rewarded by the Lord when he comes. Let us, therefore, be true to the charge he has left us because our reward will be so great, it cannot be imagined; it is more than our hearts and minds can ever comprehend.

8] We should live in expectation and anticipation of the coming of the Lord. We should ensure we line up our lives with the word of God day by day; find time to search the scriptures; fast and pray; preach the coming kingdom of God; call men to repentance and work at bringing them to the saving grace of our Lord Jesus Christ; as we await his return. What was Jesus' command? *Luke 19:13 Occupy 'til I come.*

MY TESTIMONY
ONLY JESUS COULD HELP ME
By Sister T

I had almost given up, except for the fact that I knew God was merciful. I needed the miraculous hand of God upon my life to effect any deliverance. No one else could help me. The doctors did all they knew how, without success. I kept holding on to life and believing that one day God would visit me with a miracle.

I will not attempt to give details from further back than my first marriage. We were a mixed couple. His family hated me and our lovely baby daughter so badly my husband committed suicide. I met and married my second husband a year later. God had blessed me with this wonderful man. He accepted my baby daughter as his very own.

Over a few years, I had eighteen pregnancies. I miscarried some of the babies, some were born alive but died shortly after. Others were still-born. The doctors did all they could do to help me. My daughter C was born fifteen years ago and she survived. We have two lovely daughters. We lost all the other children.

The doctors spoke to us about having a hysterectomy. We agreed and they carried out the operation. This did not go well and twenty-two more operations were to follow, over a period of fourteen years. Each operation left more illnesses and I ended up in a wheelchair with my husband having to leave his job to take care of me and our two daughters. Over the years I died on several occasions and was brought back to life with the help of machines. I was taking many tablets per day for my illnesses:

< kidney failure [I had only half kidney left]
< a heart that was in shreds and needed a transplant
< pancreas failure
< diabetes
< MRSA
< excruciating pains over the whole of my body
< hypertension
< abscesses
< oedema [excess water in my body]
< severe backache

I carried about stomas for the bowels and the bladders. I

154

had no thyroid and having had the hysterectomy, I had no womb.

These were just some of the problems, others I could not understand as a lay person. I was a total mess. I had a tube in my nose through which I was being fed. The doctors did not hold out much hope for me as the heavy medication would eventually help to finish me off. I just existed. My family did everything for me.

I did not know what it was like to play with my daughters or take them to the park. My husband learned to comb their hair and mine. He did everything. God bless him. He trusted God and believed that one day God would give us a breakthrough. Thank God for Jesus, the Lord visited us in our struggles.

Sister J from the church we used to attend seemed full of excitement/joy. Her depression and suicide tendencies seemed to have disappeared. She seemed very hopeful and happy.

Although feeling weak and helpless, I would be willing to go anywhere my husband could take me and I would be willing to try anything that might help me. "Sister J, what is it that has been happening in your life, tell me?" I said. "I have found a prayer house in Brixton, London. My sisters have old me about it. They are now saved. The anointing is powerful there and the Lord performs miracles there", she said. "You are not leaving me the next time you are going there; I need a miracle from the Lord".

Praise the Lord, we arrived safely in Brixton that Thursday evening. Apostle Lake was away. Two evangelists at the apostolic ministry prayed for me, and my husband drove me home. The Holy Spirit was powerful in the place and faith filled me. By the time I got home, I found I did not need my wheelchair and was able to walk up the stairs. I did not need the stair lift. I rang J in excitement. I did not need to wait on my husband to get me out of bed the following day. "Mother is away this week, you will see real fire when she gets back" Sister J said.

I waited excitedly for the following Thursday. Off we went to the prayer house in Brixton. Apostle Lake was back. She led the packed house in warfare prayers. It was time to pray for those who had special needs. I went forward. She asked me what was wrong. As I began to enumerate the problems she stopped me and started to pray. She laid her hand upon me and down I went. Whilst on the floor, I felt as if I was receiving an operation. When I got up I felt newness in my whole body that I had not felt for fourteen years. We went home. When I woke up the following day I found I could go into the kitchen and do the cooking. I got the laundry out and put it in the washing machine. Everyone was amazed. Since then I have got better every day. The doctors have examined me and asked who operated on my pancreas. They are amazed at what the Lord had done for me.

I can now do my house work. The two carers who used to come in the morning and in the evening to wash and dress me, have stopped coming. I can now do my shopping.

The Lord Jesus Christ has helped me and I am thanking him every day. My family are all most grateful to the Lord and we are all a part of Apostle Lake's ministry.
Thank God for the day he had us to attend the prayer

156

house. Your case is not hopeless. There is hope in God. God has effected my deliverance and if you will believe the word of God he will make the seemingly impossible situation in your life, possible. For with man it is impossible, but not with God, *"for with God nothing shall be impossible" [Luke 1:37].* God has seen your condition; you may have been waiting for many years. Do not give up, keep trusting God, he will see you through.

Blessings.

CHAPTER 13

THE END OF EVIL:[THE DEVIL, HIS DEMONS AND UNBELIEVERS]

What a glory that will be, when the ransomed home we see; What a hallelujah band, when we meet in Beulah land; What a glory that will be!

It is going to be the greatest and happiest day in the universe when satan, his demons and unbelievers are cast into the lake which burneth with fire and brimstone; when the whole universe is delivered from the wickedness of the arch-rebel called the devil and satan. Satan is doing all he can to fill up his deceit and wickedness against the human race. The earth, the firmament; everywhere the devil has set foot is contaminated with sin and darkness. The earth and its inhabitants, which he hates bitterly, is reeling under the weight of sin and the consequences of sin, but the arch-rebel's time is nearly up. He is moving fast these days because he knows he has but a short time. He is making a fast last minute grab to drag as many as possible down into the pit with him and his princes of darkness. However, his end is imminent; his doom is settled and there is nothing he can do about it. He is going to have to bow to the Christ of God whom he hates with a bitter hatred. Let us have a look at what is coming to him soon.

Revelation 6:12-17 12. And I beheld when he had opened the sixth seal, and lo, there was a great earthquake; and the sun became black as sackcloth of hair, and the moon became as blood; 13. And the stars of heaven fell unto

158

the earth, even as a fig tree casteth her untimely figs, when she is shaken of a mighty wind. 14. And the heaven departed as a scroll when it is rolled together; and every mountain and island were moved out of their places. 15. And the kings of the earth, and the great men, and the rich men, and the chief captains, and the mighty men, and every bondman, and every free man, hid themselves in the dens and in the rocks of the mountains. 16. And said to the mountains and rocks, Fall on us, and hide us from the face of him that sitteth on the throne, and from the wrath of the Lamb. 17. For the great day of his wrath is come; and who shall be able to stand?

We find many who, although sinful, know how good and kind Jesus is and they refuse to believe that a holy and loving heavenly Father could throw them into the fires of hell. Here is news for those who do not believe this truth; Yes, hell was made for the devil and his demons *[Matthew 25:41 - depart from me ye cursed, into everlasting fire, prepared for the devil and his angels.]* but is ready to receive all wicked and rebellious humans, who will be thrown into the fire. The bible talks about a great earthquake. The recent terrible earthquakes, e.g in Japan and elsewhere will be almost a joke to what is to come at the end of the age; then there will be stars falling from heaven; the sun becoming black and the moon becoming blood. The heavens will open up to let out the mighty and all-powerful Lord Jesus Christ as he comes down to do judgment. All the great people of earth; the oppressors, the rich people and the world leaders who rule with rigour will find themselves hiding from the holy presence of our blessed Lord. The servants and slaves who did not accept Jesus as their Lord and saviour will be severely punished because Jesus took delight in preaching the gospel to the poor.

God does not want people to suffer in this life and end up in eternal fire when he comes.

When Jesus comes the second time, he is not coming to save people; he has already done that. He is coming to judge and punish those who have been disobedient to his word; those who have sided with satan and his demons to rebel against his righteous ways.

Revelation 12:9-10 *9. And the great dragon was cast out, that old serpent, called the devil, and satan, which deceiveth the whole world: he was cast out into the earth, and his angels were cast out with him. 10. And I heard a loud voice saying in heaven, Now is come salvation, and strength, and the kingdom of our God, and the power of his Christ: for the accuser of our brethren is cast down, which accused them before our God day and night. 11. And they overcame him by the blood of the Lamb, and by the word of their testimony; and they loved not their lives unto the death.*

All those dear saints who have been accused by satan and who have overcome him by the word of their testimony and by the precious blood of Jesus, will see the end of that wicked one. Satan was cast out of heaven and he dragged down with him a third of the angels. This arch deceiver is a liar and the father of lies. Let us walk uprightly and his lies will be of no avail. The sinful inhabitants of earth will try hiding from the presence of the Lord when he comes, but I am not sure whether satan and his demons will even be allowed to hide. They must squarely face up to their wickedness in the presence of the Lord. They must face the fires of hell, smell it and dwell in it.

Revelation 19:19-20 *19. And I saw the beast, and the*

160

kings of the earth, and their armies, gathered together to make war against him that sat on the horse, and against his army. 20. And the beast was taken, and with him the false prophet that wrought miracles before him, with which he deceived them that had received the mark of the beast, and them that worshipped his image. These both were cast alive into a lake of fire burning with brimstone.

Yes! satan and those who serve him will make a last minute bid to take over the kingdom of the Lord. The devil will deceive himself even to the end, but the bible says that he and the false prophet which wrought miracles were cast into the lake of fire. Satan has already lost every fight. He lost at Calvary's cross. Jesus paid the price for man's disobedience but satan refuses to give up. Beware of him; he will fight until he is thrown into the fires of hell.

Revelation 20:10-15 *10. And the devil that deceived them was cast into the lake of fire and brimstone, where the beast and false prophet are, and shall be tormented day and night for ever and ever. 11. And I saw a great white throne, and him that sat on it, from whose face the earth and the heaven fled away; and there was found no place for them. 12. And I saw the dead, small and great, stand before God; and the books were opened: and another book was opened, which is the book of life: and the dead were judged out of those things which were written in the books, according to their works. 13. And the sea gave up the dead which were in it; and death and hell delivered up the dead which were in them; and they were judged every man according to their works. 14. And death and hell were cast into the lake of fire. This is the second death. 15. And whosoever was not found written in the book of life was cast into the lake of fire.*

This is all about fire! Firstly, the beast and the false prophet will be cast into the fires of hell. That is, the worldly kingdom and the false church found their way into the lake of fire. Now it was time for satan to join them; that instigator of evil. The bible says that every one was judged according to their works; they were judged out of the books. Why? Because all that we do here, good or bad, is recorded in heaven and will meet us at the judgment. Time is winding up, so we had better make sure we are having some good things in the book of life, not in those books. It is amazing that those who asked for watery graves will come up out of the sea. The sea will just give them up to be judged. Every one of the creation of God will be obedient to the word of the Lord and will release their dead to face the judgment of the Lord for all their deeds. The state of death and the grave will be cast into the fire. In the Lord's holy kingdom there will be no death. There will be no need for death, because death is a curse and there will be only blessings in the kingdom of God. Who else gets thrown into hell? All disobedient and rebellious people. Satan will not be able to help you on the day of judgment. Leave him alone and turn to Christ. Jesus died for you and for me. There is a great day coming for all: great and glorious for the redeemed; great and bitter for the deceived ones.

Revelation 21:8 *But the fearful and unbelieving, and the abominable, and murderers, and whoremongers, and sorcerers, and idolaters, and all liars, shall have their part in the lake which burneth with fire and brimstone: which is the second death.*

Fear is the opposite of faith. Those who have not put their trust in the Lord will walk in fear instead of faith. To get to heaven we must put our trust in the completed work of

Christ, walk in faith and avail ourselves of all Jesus has accomplished for us and receive his salvation. Those unbelievers who have not done this are on their way to hell. And what about the murderers? Those who walk in hate instead of love; in unforgiveness instead of forgiveness? They follow on into the fire where the unbelievers, the abominable and the murderers are. The sexually immoral and those who cover up for them will also find themselves in hell. Today, sin seems to be not sin at all. Sin seems to be just another lifestyle and we have to be very careful how we even mention some words. Christians are being asked to accept sin and not see it for what it is – destructive. God hates sorcery and idolatry because both are of the devil. To indulge in sorcery/witchcraft is to be involved in devil worship, the worship of another god and the rejection of the true and living Christ. This provokes the Lord to anger, yet even the Lord's people are being pushed by the world's system to accept these evils as normal. We will not accept them! *Exodus 20:3 Thou shalt have no other gods before me.*

The world at large needs to know what is good and right in the eyes of the Lord and repent and turn to Jesus. Man was made for God's glory, not for devil worship. Liars? All liars shall go straight to hell. The world system is built on lies. In society, people are expected to lie to get by, but the Lord's people will stand firm upon the truth. There are all sorts of lies: There are the general type of lies; saying you don't know when you do know; saying something that is definitely not so; and there is the deceiver: he pretends to be what he is not. I will stop here because *all* liars shall have their part in the lake which burneth with fire and brimstone. Why does Jesus hate lies so much? Jesus hates lies because this opposes truth and satan is the author of lies. The devil is the enemy of righteousness. Satan's power is in the lies he tells; the deceit he holds to; all geared to lead people away from Jesus [the truth].

This is where the gospel [good news] comes in and is most necessary. The gospel of Jesus Christ teaches man to do good. The gospel gives man the opportunity to turn away from evil. Man needs to repent and turn to the Lord who will save him and change him from the inside. Man needs God if he is to escape the damnation of hell. Hell was made by God for the devil and his angels, not for man.

There is coming soon, the time when satan and his evil workers will be cast into hell, where their worm dieth not, and the fire is not quenched. Little does satan and his emissaries know that they are fulfilling prophecy and hastening the coming of the Lord. However, The Lord's people are awaiting that day when sin and satan will be no more.

In Summary

1] The end of all things is at hand. The heavens will depart as a scroll and all the great people of earth, rich men, rulers, employers and servants will all run to the rocks and mountains for cover as they flee from the presence of the Lord. They will be seeking a place to hide from the wrath of the Lamb of God.

2] Satan was cast out of heaven and thrown down to the earth where he deceives great and small.

3] The beast and the false prophet [the wicked world rulership and the false religious system] will be cast into the lake of fire. These enemies of righteousness will disappear for ever.

4] The judgment is set. Satan and his demons will be cast into the lake of fire, where the beast and false prophet already are. The dead, small and great, will stand before the Judge of all the earth and they will be judged of all their evil deeds which they have wickedly committed. They will be judged out of the books, every man according to his works. Death and hell will deliver up their dead and they will all appear before the Lord at the judgment. All the wicked will be cast into the lake of fire, burning with brimstone. Both the state of death and hell will be cast into the lake of fire. Fire! Fire! Fire! for satan and his cohorts and for all those who disobey God and follow the deceitfulness of sin and satan. This will be the end of the wicked.

5] Every one should look up to the higher powers in Christ Jesus and the nations should aim at submitting their lives to the Lord. Hell is a terrible place and Jesus died to prevent man ending up there. Hell was made for the devil and his angels; it was not made for man. Satan is the originator of sin, why does man want to end up where he goes?

6] There is no repentance in the grave and nothing can be done for people who end up at the Judgment Seat of Christ to give every man account to God of all the deeds he has committed in his earthly life. No excuses will be accepted since man has the gospel here to believe and accept. Man will be judged, not for what he has done, [wrong attitude and behaviour]; he will be judged for what he has not done. He will be judged for not accepting Jesus as his personal saviour and Lord.

7]   Accept Jesus Christ as your Lord and saviour and escape the damnation of hell. This is the final destination of the rebellious and disobedient. If you do not know Jesus as your Lord and saviour, turn to him before it is too late.

MY TESTIMONY – HOW THE LORD DELIVERED ME WHILST ON THE MISSION FIELD
By Dr Lake

It does not matter where you are, God is there. Jesus said, "And lo I am with you always, even unto the end of the world. *[Matthew 28:20].* I was at the end of the world all right; I was in the Philippines. It took us at least eighteen hours flight by aircraft. With the road journey to where we would stay, we were travelling for at least twenty four hours.

We ministered from place to place: crusades, seminars, general services where I did much ministry work and saw multitudes both saved and healed. We were scheduled to do ministry work on this trip for one month and everything went well. The Lord magnified his holy name in all the places where we went. Souls were healed, delivered and filled with the Holy Ghost. We travelled over hills and valleys, in sunshine and rain, but God blessed his work through us. I brought deeper light and truth to many ministers and our ministry was very fruitful. Churches were in the planting, for the glory of the Lord. Our ministers were wonderful people. The trip had nearly come to an end. We were due to leave tomorrow. On our mission trips it is normal practice to take care of the food for all the ministers who travel up and down with us. We mostly live in rented houses in which we sometimes hold seminars providing the accommodation is large enough, although sometimes we have had to stay in hotels, if they were not able to find an appropriate house for us to rent. The ministers and leaders would come round and we would provide for them. On this particular day, the day before we were due to leave for home, many ministers had come to the hotel where we were staying. Since we had been spending a lot of money we had almost run out. However, I was very hungry and decided that myself and Pastor Fred, my mission co-worker would leave the ministers in my hotel room and pop down to the local restaurant and get something to eat. We did not ask any of them to accompany us because we had very little money and this would not be sufficient to feed us and them. Off we went and stopped at the nearest cafe/restaurant. There was a lot of food displayed ready to be eaten. I filled up my plate with as many things as my plate could hold, including some sea weed. Pastor Fred bought only rolls and pepsi. I ate as much as I could [I was famished!]. Whilst I was eating though, something did not taste very nice, but I just continued to eat. We were not very long, and returned to the hotel. I continued to speak with the ministers and discussed various matters relating to this mission work.

It was time for them to go to their various homes and we said good night. "See you in the morning". I told them the time we would be boarding the plane. Pastor Fred went to his room and I got ready for bed. About mid-night I did not feel well at all and my stomach felt very upset. Then came the stomach ache. The pain with the stomach ache was excruciating. I realised that I had had food poisoning. I started to rush to the toilet and I had to make it real fast. This was accompanied by vomiting. I was very poisoned and I was ill. I went to the room of Pastor Fred and knocked. He opened the door and I said, "I have food poisoning – I am really ill". I had to dash back to the toilet and again the pain was becoming unbearable. In these places it is not easy to get hold of a doctor quickly. Pastor Fred followed behind me to my room, whilst I ran into the toilet. I began to become weak. Pastor Fred began to pray. He prayed, and prayed, and prayed. As he prayed I felt like I was surrounded by complete peace. He stopped for a minute. This felt as if something had been lost, so I said, please continue to pray. This he did and he pressed on with the prayers. To the Lord be all the glory and praise, the stomach pain ceased and the diarrhoea and vomiting disappeared. No more pain; it was all gone. Jesus had healed me. I was able to go to sleep and was up and well the next morning ready to leave for home. Jesus Christ is the only and great healer who followed us to the Philippines; took care of us; healed and delivered me from the plans of the devil. I thought of what could have happened, had it not been for the miracle working power of the Lord. I could have ended up in a hospital in the Philippines; I might have had to delay my flight and possibly have had to pay more money for my flight.

We can trust the Lord to take care of us at home and abroad. We may rest assured that he will look after us even in a foreign land. Jesus would never send us out on mission and leave us alone. God is faithful and Jesus is precious.

If you feel that the Lord is sending you on the mission

field, be obedient and go; Jesus will take care of you. You can depend on him to honour his word. "I am with you always, even unto the end of the world". *[Matthew 28:20].*

CHAPTER 14

THE THINGS WHICH GOD HAS PREPARED FOR THEM THAT LOVE HIM

It is with great excitement that I set out to write this chapter. Hear this: *1 Corinthians 2:9 But as it is written, Eye hath not seen, nor ear heard, neither have entered into the heart of man, the things which God hath prepared for them that love him.* We, mortals, will never be able to even guess at what God has prepared for those of us who love him. Our hard work, our labour, our hurts, our pain and suffering, the attacks of evil men, the persecution, the closed doors to the Lord's word [this can be quite hurtful to those of us who set out to promulgate the gospel], the self denial, the hard trials at home and abroad, and much more, will seem light affliction when we see Jesus in all his glory; when we are receiving our crown of life which will never fade away. What can I say saints except to encourage you with a few lines of the word of this song: Press along saints, press along;   It's God's own way; Press along saints, press along;   It's God's own way; Persecution we must bear; Trials and crosses in the way; But the hotter the battle; The sweeter the victory. Another songwriter says: When we all see Jesus; We'll sing and shout the victory. When all our trials and troubles are over; we will meet Jesus on that beautiful shore.

I have just been trying to see if I can capture what we can expect but it is not coming off well so I will go to the scripture.

1 Corinthians 2:9-10   9. But as it is written, Eye hath not seen, nor ear heard, neither have entered into the heart of man, the things which God hath prepared for them that love him.   10. But God hath revealed them unto us by his Spirit: for the Spirit searcheth all things, yea, the deep things of God.

Here the bible says that the things God has prepared for us who love him has never entered into our hearts, yet the word goes on to say that God has revealed these things to us by his Spirit. Well, we just cannot express it. We can feel the sweetness in our souls, and the songwriter says this love and blessing makes us laugh and it makes us cry, but it is far above what we can express. We can feel it in our spirits but we just cannot imagine what these blessings will look like, all we can do is keep rejoicing in this great truth.

*Isaiah **65:17**   For, behold, I create new heavens and a new earth: and the former shall not be remembered.*

Praise the Lord, in the new earth the former things shall not be remembered. The things that used to disturb us and make us unhappy and sad, will all be completely forgotten. What a joy that will be, just to have things working smoothly all the time. O, how we struggle to get things running smoothly. It is prayer and more prayer to keep the demons out of our affairs: to keep our children from getting into trouble; just to hold down our jobs, to be at peace with our neighbours; to receive healing for the sicknesses and diseases. Then there are the seemingly ordinary things like being late for work; missing the bus; the nagging feeling that the traffic warden might have given us a ticket; and worse yet, someone we love dying and leaving our homes lonely and sad. Hallelujah, there will be no more sadness and we will forget all those evil things that took place in our earthly sojourn. We anticipate that great day.

Revelation 19:5-9, 11, 16 *5. And a voice came out of the throne, saying, Praise our God, all ye his servants, and ye that fear him, both small and great. 6. And I heard as it were the voice of a great multitude, and as the voice of many waters, and as the voice of mighty thundering, saying, Alleluia: for the Lord God omnipotent reigneth. 7. Let us be glad and rejoice, and give honour to him: for the marriage of the Lamb is come, and his wife hath made herself ready. 11. And I saw heaven opened, and behold a white horse; and he that sat upon him was called Faithful and True, and in righteousness, he doth judge and make war. 16. And he hath on his vesture and on his thigh a name written, KING OF KINGS, AND LORD OF LORDS.*

This is a time of praise and worship; no more sorrow, no more sighing, no more problems, no more tears, no more sadness. The former things have passed away. There will be many of us there. The multitude of the redeemed will be like the voice of many waters and as the voice of mighty thunderings. Together we will be singing the praises: Alleluia: the Lord God omnipotent reigneth. Yes, our God reigns. He is all mighty. It is gladness time, a time of rejoicing when the Lord's people give him all the honour and praise, for he is worthy. O glorious Jesus. What a joyous time that is going to be when our Faithful and True Lord steps out to judge the world and shows his greatness to his people who adore him: KING OF KINGS AND LORD OF LORDS. He is above all and we just fall down now and worship. He is our wonderful saviour who has brought us into this great victory by the power of his precious blood. Thank you Jesus. You will be most beautiful to behold.

Revelation 21:1-5, 23-27 [please read the whole chapter]
1. And I saw a new heaven and a new earth: for the first heaven and the first earth were passed away; and there was no more sea. 2. And I John saw the holy city, new Jerusalem, coming down from God out of heaven, prepared as a bride adorned for her husband. 3. And I heard a great voice out of heaven saying, Behold, the tabernacle of God is with men, and he will dwell with them, and they shall be his people, and God himself shall be with them, and be their God. 4. And God shall wipe away all tears from their eyes; and there shall be no more death, neither sorrow, nor crying, neither shall there be any more pain: for the former things are passed away. 5. And he that sat upon the throne said, Behold, I make all things new. And he said unto me, Write: for these words are true and faithful. 23. And the city had no need of the sun, neither of the moon, to shine in it: for the glory of God did lighten it, and the Lamb is the light thereof. 24. And the nations of them which are saved shall walk in the light of it: and the kings of the earth do bring their glory and honour into it. 25. And the gates of it shall not be shut at all by day; for there shall be no night there. 26. And they shall bring the glory and honour of the nations into it. 27. And there shall in no wise enter into it any thing that defileth, neither whatsoever worketh abomination, or maketh a lie: but they which are written in the Lamb's book of life.

This earth on which we live is, in these days, very terrible, full of distress and every evil thing, but the Lord has promised us a new heaven and a new earth; this old world system will pass away and the holy city, new Jerusalem will come down from heaven, as beautiful as a bride dressed up for her husband. Thank God, there will be no more tears, no more crying, no more pain, no more death

173

[that evil enemy]. Every evil thing will disappear for ever and God will make all things new, praise the Lord. I sigh with relief as I write this. Those dark, dull nights will be a thing of the past, never to terrify the redeemed again and we shall walk in the light of God's glory. Since there will be no more warmongers, no thieves, no wicked people, no obnoxious demons, there will be no need for walls of protection and gates will not be locked to keep out the wicked. What blessedness! O Lord, I anticipate that wonderful day. Come quickly Lord Jesus.

Revelation 22:1-6, 12-14 And he showed me a pure river of water of life, clear as crystal, proceeding out of the throne of God and of the Lamb. 2. In the midst of the street of it, and on either side of the river, was there the tree of life, which bare twelve manner of fruits, and yielded her fruit every month: and the leaves of the tree were for the healing of the nations. 3. And there shall be no more curse: but the throne of God and of the Lamb shall be in it, and his servants shall serve him: 4. And they shall see his face; and his name shall be in their foreheads. 5. And there shall be no night there; and they need no candle, neither light of the sun; for the Lord God giveth them light: and they shall reign for ever and ever. 6. And he said unto me, These sayings are faithful and true: and the Lord God of the holy prophets sent his angel to shew unto his servants the things which must shortly be done. 12. And, behold I come quickly; and my reward is with me, to give every man according as his work shall be. 13. I am Alpha and Omega, the beginning and the end, the first and the last. 14. Blessed are they that do his commandments, that they may have right to the tree of life, and may enter in through the gates into the city.

Thank God we shall be beside the water of life, close to

the tree of life. Adam and Eve were driven out of the garden of Eden so they would not eat of the tree of life and live miserably for ever. Now we are at the place where we can be by the tree of life. Away with curse, there shall be no more of it. We shall look upon the face of our saviour and his name shall be written on our foreheads. I am not going to ponder whether this will be physically or spiritually because I will be living in the realm of the Spirit of the Lord anyway.

Hear this: The glory of the Lord will lighten this glorious city and we will need no electric lights; the sun will not need to give us light because our heavenly Father will be our light there. These things will surely come to pass and we, the Lord's people, are looking forward to them.

And regarding the coming of the Lord? Jesus has warned us: ***Behold I come quickly.*** He has told us in his word that at his coming he will reward every man according as his work shall be. Let us do good works because we will be rewarded by the Lord. There is a blessing for those who obey the commandments of God. We will have a right to the tree of life and will enter through the gates into the holy city. Heaven awaits the righteous, heaven awaits the faithful and where Jesus is, it is heaven there. There have been all sorts of controversy about where the saints will be when the Lord comes. I am not bothered about that. I will be where Jesus is because he has promised that he will come and receive us unto himself. Is that not good enough? That is enough for me.

In Summary:

1] The end of all things is at hand. There is a great day coming when the Lord's people who have been faithful;

who have been obedient to his word; who have made full proof of their ministry, and who have endured to the end; will receive a crown of life which fadeth not away.

2]   God will make a new heaven and a new earth and this old system of things with all its wickedness will surely pass away and we shall live in the light of the presence of the Lord.

3]   In the new system of things which the Lord our saviour shall give us, there shall be no more pain, no more sorrow, no more suffering, no more crying, and no more death. All these shall come to an end and God's people will enjoy their Lord securely and joyfully. There shall be peace for evermore.

4] These great blessings are for those who do the commandments of the Lord; who are obedient to his word; who occupy until he comes; who are faithful and endure unto the end.

5]   Have a look at the state of evil men! They are outside the gates of heaven, outside the beautiful city. ***Revelation 22:15*** *For without are dogs and sorcerers, and whoremongers, and murderers, and idolaters, and whosoever loveth and maketh a lie.*

6]   What should man do to enter God's holy kingdom and avoid the second resurrection? He should prepare to meet his God. ***Amos 4:12***.

7]   There is going to be a first resurrection for the righteous, and a second resurrection for the wicked. The righteous will enter the pearly gates, the wicked, hell fire. ***Admonition:*** Let us not be weary in well doing, for in

176

due season, we shall reap if we faint not.*[Galatians 6:9]*. Let us keep our eyes on the Lord Jesus and anticipate his imminent return to free his saints from this evil system of things.

MY TESTIMONY OF VICTORY
By Sister A H

Jesus is my deliverer. Firstly, I was never brought up in church, but attended occasionally. I got to know many bible stories. I knew that God was my Creator; that he knows everything and that he sees every thing. I can remember as far back as the age of 5-6. I suffered from terrible nightmares and often felt as if I was being held down in my sleep.

One day I was talking to my cousin who is just a few months younger, about my dreams, and he told me to ask God not to make me dream. He said God would stop me from dreaming and from being afraid. I did that. When I was going to bed I would pray little prayers taught me by my mother and then I would repeat the words, "Please God, don't let me dream, but let me breathe". As a child, I believed that I would die in my sleep. Having said this over and over again I would make up stores in my head to put myself to sleep. My stories would be about angels playing with children in heaven and how beautiful that is. I did this for years.

As I got older and was becoming an adult I saw the world as not a very nice place and when things got hard for me I would suffer from depression. When this happened, I would go back to the stories I used to make up about angels when I was a child. However, this no longer

177

worked for me and I would lapse into complete blankness and darkness and would just cry and cry. I would just want the world to stop. My family were very supportive and took me to the doctors, but they did not seem to be able to help me and I was going through life with sadness resting upon my heart. I felt as though something was missing in my life.

In 2009 the depression got worse and there was a time when I was afraid to leave the house. One day I went shopping, and for some reason I was in a book store looking for a book on Angels that I could read, but I ended up buying a book called "Conversation with God". The Lord knew why I was buying this book. It was a great book and from then on I started my own conversations with the Lord. Whenever I found I had done wrong I would go to the Lord for forgiveness. My relationship with God became very real and he became my real and best friend.

Although God was now my friend, I would not go to church because I was not sure which church would be the right one for me; I also believed that many of the churches were not right. However, I wanted to learn more about God and I asked him to lead me to the right church, so when a friend invited me to a prayer meeting in her house I decided to go because she was a good friend and I wanted to give her my support, also I wanted to be built up in prayer because I was not praying properly as I was feeling rather low. I believe the devil was holding me back since as I was going to travel the next day, I felt that I needed to get my daughter's hair done in thin twist which would last us whilst we were away. This meant I was going to have to stay at home. I started to twist my daughter's hair; I had done only about three twists when I felt the need to go to the prayer meeting. I left off combing my daughter's hair and asked the Lord to help me to finish off what I had to do when I returned, including my daughter's hair, because I had to go to the prayer meeting.

I went to the prayer meeting and met Apostle Lake. As we prayed and studied the word of God, I became so excited at her knowledge of the word that I did not want the meeting to end. I felt that I needed to take her home with me. God had heard my prayer. When I returned from the prayer meeting, I found that my cousin had come round to my home and finished off my daughter's hair for me.

From that day, I have tried my best to attend the prayer meetings and church services. With the help of one of the saints I surrendered my heart to the Lord. I got baptized; my depression has gone; my heart is full of the joy of the Lord; I am no longer bound, I can pray; I have a hunger for the word of God and I am reading and studying my bible; I have peace and I give God all the glory for bringing me to him and giving me what I really needed: JESUS.

If you are in a situation like the one I was in, come to the Lord now and receive his love and peace. Your depression will go when the love of Christ comes in and you will have the joy that I have. Please do not remain in that awful situation of hopelessness, Jesus is ready to set you free. Find a church to attend and call upon his Name.

May God's blessings rest upon you.

CONCLUSION

In writing this book I have endeavoured to share with the church of the Lord Jesus Christ the imminence of his return, as we see prophecy concerning his second coming being fulfilled before our eyes. I have, from scripture pointed the reader to the fact that the prophecies regarding the Lord's first coming were fulfilled and he came into the world to save sinners and restore man to the first dominion.

Many of the prophecies concerning the Lord's second coming have been fulfilled and it is certain that the rest will be fulfilled. From scripture we see that we are in the end of the age. The church, and indeed the world should be prepared for the coming of the Lord. It is high time that the church search the scriptures and walk in line with the word of God. Many areas of Christendom have long been backslidden and should go back to revealed truth and walk therein.

There is shortly to be the midnight cry when many Christians will find themselves short of the Lord's divine requirements of holiness and since, *"without holiness no man shall see the Lord" [Hebrews 12:14],* some will hear the words, *"Depart from me ye cursed into everlasting fire" [Matthew 25:41].* May this not be our portion, in Jesus' name.

As the church eagerly awaits the soon return of the Lord, she should go all out to pluck some out of the fire. The Lord has given the church power to release the captives out of the prison house of sin and satan and to minister the word of God to them so that they may enter into eternal life.

This is not the time to remain in a lukewarm state; it is time to fast and pray and seek the Lord; time to minister the word of God to a word hungry and sin sick world. World leaders have led their subjects astray with deceitful laws; the holy scriptures have been thrown aside and substituted with man-made rules and humanism. The church should be praying for a revival of the truth of God's word to deliver the souls of men.

My prayer is that Christians everywhere will stand together in these last and final days of earth's history and act upon the following word of God: *Jeremiah 1:10 See, I have this day set thee over the nations and over the kingdoms, to root out, and to pull down, and to destroy, and to throw down, to build, and to plant.*

May the Lord help his people to be ready when he comes; and may the Lord help the unsaved to understand the signs of the times and repent and turn to God.

Bottom Line:
Ecclesiastes 12:13-14 Let us hear the conclusion of the whole matter: Fear God and keep his commandments: for this is the whole duty of man. For God shall bring every work into judgment, with every secret thing, whether it be good, or whether it be evil.

Apostle Dr Daisy Lake

APPENDIX 1

TESTIMONIES

HOW JESUS REVEALED TO ME
THE POWER IN HIS BLOOD
By Dr Daisy Lake

I promised the Lord that whenever and wherever there was an opportunity I would testify of how he brought back my son from the dead by the revelation of the all powerful blood of Jesus Christ, and I will do so here.

Leviticus 17:11 For the life of the flesh is in the blood: and I have given it to you upon the altar to make an atonement for your souls; for it is the blood that maketh an atonement for the soul.

It was a very bleak and chilly day, winter lingered on. My son came in from work as usual, ready to take me shopping. "Conrad, I said, there is no need for you to take me shopping today, I will go to the local shop and ask them to deliver the shopping for me". "That's OK Mummy", he said, and I went off.

I had been living in the area for many years and normally I would meet up and talk with people known to me for a long time. However, it was fairly cold and I needed to go to the toilet so I did the shopping quickly, asked the shopkeeper to deliver and rushed home. When I got home, although I needed very much to go to the toilet, I had thought of stopping in the kitchen downstairs and of taking some fish out of the fridge that I had planned to cook that evening. The urgency of using the toilet prevented me from going into the kitchen and I ran upstairs.

My son was doing shift work at the time and he had a bath whenever he came in from work. I could smell the use of the bath. [The bath and the toilet were in the same room]. For years we had talked of putting another toilet downstairs but it never came to fruition. Thank God it didn't. Sometimes when things do not seem to be going the way we would like them to go, we should remember that *all things work together for good to those who love the Lord. [Romans 8:28].*

I knocked at the bathroom door, "open the door please" I said. I heard a groaning sound. "Are you constipated, open the door please". I was desperate. He undid the lock and I went into the bathroom. I had no plans for what I saw. My son was propped up against the wall, eyes closed. I thought he must have had a heart attack. I decided quickly to ring a Christian sister who was not working at the time and ask her to come and help whilst I call the doctor. A voice spoke to me very audibly, "there is no time for the doctor". God was on my case. I turned round quickly and the Holy Spirit took control. I grabbed hold of my son and cried out, "Jesus help me, Lord you have to help me now". It was a loud cry of distress. I felt the power of God overshadow me and I began to minister in the Lord's power. "Spirit of death, loose him, you can't have him, hand him over to me in Jesus' name". The words were being put in my mouth, they were definitely not rehearsed because I did not expect what I found. I began to plead the blood of Jesus very loudly, "the blood of Jesus, the blood of Jesus, the blood of Jesus". I pleaded the blood of Jesus until I began to say, "blood, blood, blood". The voice said to me "the blood of

183

Jesus". Conrad stood on his feet. I began to say "Conrad, tell me what happened". The words had hardly left my mouth when he collapsed on me and his eyes closed. This was a tough spiritual battle the Lord was taking me through. I fought, using the blood of Jesus. I pleaded the blood of Jesus with all my heart. The anointing was heavy on me; I felt like rain was falling on me. I took hold of Conrad's face and laid my hand on his forehead to pray for him, but as I did this, his face shook as though one was shaking fruits off a tree. Once again he stood upright but this time he was saying, "the blood of Jesus, the blood of Jesus, the blood of Jesus". I continued to plead the blood of Jesus, I was not taking any chances in case he slipped away again. I was making sure he had fully recovered.

As I continued to plead the blood of Jesus on the top of my voice, my son said, "Mummy, I am all right now". "The blood of Jesus", I said. "Honestly, I am all right Mum". I continued pleading the blood of Jesus until I felt in my spirit that the Lord was through with the miracle he was performing.

I again said, "Conrad, tell me what happened". The bath was still full of water and he was naked. We let the water out, he put his clothes on, and here is the story:

After I had left the house to do the shopping, he went to have his usual bath. The bathroom was cold and the water for his bath was fairly hot. The bathroom was showing signs of condensation and he had opened the window to let the steam out. Whilst he was in the bath he was praying. He thought his ears were filling up with water and he leaned over to each side to shake any water out. Nothing came out of either ear. The vehicles passing near our home sounded miles away. Things did not seem normal. He said, "Father, what's happening here". He came out of the bath. By then his ears had completely blocked up. He saw what looked like a casket come from above and it covered him. The casket was transparent. He saw me come into the bathroom but the casket separated him from me and he was unable to communicate with me. He slipped out of his body at a very high speed and travelled upward so fast that by the time I started pleading the blood of Jesus he must have been thousands of miles out in space. I told Conrad I had been binding the spirit of death. He said the only words he heard were "the blood of Jesus". He said, "You stopped pleading the blood of Jesus at one time because I seemed to have travelled even faster when you stopped". I said, "it would have been the time when I thought you had come round".

Conrad said that first, as I pleaded the blood of Jesus, he heard it very faintly and it began to pull him back. As he came back a bit closer to earth he heard it a little louder. He said, as I continued to plead the blood of Jesus it dragged him back step by step. It was like a cord pulling him back until it pulled him right back into his body.

"How did you get into the bathroom Mummy", he asked. I said, "you opened the door". "I couldn't have done", he said. "Well, the Holy Ghost did", I replied.

As I came back to myself, I stood at the bathroom door wondering what had happened. The voice of the Lord spoke to me again, "That is how you are to minister to Karen". Karen is my youngest daughter. She was in primary school at the time and had had an infection in her stomach. I was looking to the Lord to heal her. I had prayed for her many times over three weeks and it would not go. She screamed in pain day and night. She just cried when she came in from school. A few days before Conrad's miracle I rang the doctor and made an appointment to take Karen to see her. I reasoned that the Lord was not healing her, as perhaps he wanted me to take her to the doctor so he could do something special that I had not seen before. She was in a lot of pain and I decided that it would not be fair on the child to wait any longer for a miracle.

The Lord was going to do a miracle. I took Karen from school that evening and I laid my hand on her stomach and pleaded the blood of Jesus: "the blood of Jesus, the blood of Jesus, the blood of Jesus". I pleaded the blood of Jesus for what must have been the best part of an hour. She went to the toilet and shouted, "Mummy, my stomach ache has gone". She was very excited, praise the Lord. Jesus is the truth.

The Lord then said to me, "I have given you the blood". I have taken it and I use it for everything. There is power in the blood of Jesus. Before that day, I knew very little about the power over the devil's work when the blood of Jesus is appropriated. I knew that Jesus had shed his blood to take away the sins of the human race, but I did not know much more about the precious blood of Jesus. The church I went to was a small Pentecostal church where we learned only the basics of Christianity. On this particular day God revealed the importance of the blood of Jesus in our Christian walk.

For a whole week after that miraculous day, I woke up at about 5.00 am and read all the Psalms of thanksgiving and praise. I praised God for hours and gave him thanks for his love and for the power of his blood. I thought of how

I would have been organizing my son's funeral and I gave Jesus all the thanks in the universe. The Psalms helped me to praise the Lord because I could not find words to adore and thank and praise the Lord enough.

I received a revelation of the blood of Jesus on that day of miracles and I have gone on to learn more as the Lord opens up my understanding and reveals scripture on the blood of Jesus. I have done studies on the blood of Jesus and continue to do so. The Lord is using the ministry on the blood of Jesus to scatter demons, heal bodies, clean up homes, etc. Plead the blood of Jesus. The devil and his demons do not like when the church sounds out the blood of Jesus, it cripples them.

The revelation Jesus gave me of the power in his blood came through a very hard experience, but it was well worth it. The life of the flesh is in the blood and as I pleaded the blood of Jesus, it gave life to my son.

As I share what the Lord has revealed to me on the blood of Jesus and what he is revealing, I trust all who read this testimony will get all their needs met as they learn to plead the blood of Jesus.

Remember, when those demons come to steal your sweet sleep, plead the blood of Jesus; when your children are in trouble, plead the blood of Jesus; when you have lost your job and do not know what to do, plead the blood of Jesus; when you have no money, plead the blood of Jesus; when temptations are rushing in on you, plead the blood of Jesus; when you are travelling and you need God's protection, plead the blood of Jesus; when you feel lonely and it seems no one cares, plead the blood of Jesus; when the evil system in which we live seems to be getting on top of you, plead the blood of Jesus; before you study your lessons, plead the blood of Jesus; when you need revelation of the word of God, plead the blood of Jesus; if you fall down, plead the blood of Jesus; if you are sick, plead the blood of Jesus; when you can't go to sleep, plead the blood of Jesus; when bad news reach you, plead the blood of Jesus. What can I more say? Plead the blood of Jesus in every situation, it works every time.

MY TESTIMONY: HOW THE LORD DELIVERED ME IN CHILDBIRTH
By Pastor RL

Psalm 46: *God is our refuge and strength, a very present help in trouble.*

It was December 14th, 2004 when I went into hospital for the birth of my fourth child. The year before that I had given birth to my third child by Caesarean section. On arriving at the hospital, I was advised that I should have a Caesarean section because it was so soon after the birth of my third child. The usual preparation for the operation was done and I was told that it would take twenty minutes. Shortly after, I developed complications. As soon as I was given the injection to numb my lower body, excruciating pain set in and my hands became numb and began to turn black. I screamed in pain. I was told that I was being hysterical, that I should calm down and everything would be over shortly. However, the pain became worse.

When they opened me up, they found that my womb had attached itself to my internal organs whilst healing from my last Caesarean and they weren't able to get the baby out. After an hour and a half of trying to get the baby out, and with an extensive loss of blood, they sent for the Consultant who took forty-five minutes to come. When he arrived, he managed to get the baby out. By this time, I had been opened up for almost three hours. I felt my body going into shock, my lips began to swell, my hands were black and I was drifting in and out of consciousness. I kept remembering a dream I had the night before where an angel told me that I was going to have a baby boy and he gave me a name for the baby. I comforted myself with this dream knowing that God would deliver me. The pain was so intense, I could not speak, and felt as though my chest was exploding. I tried to get up to see if they would understand the extent of the pain. I was pushed back down on the trolley. I began to plead the blood of Jesus, even in my delirium. I was calling my mum and looking around for her. I heard the Consultant telling them to close me up as quickly as possible and asking them why they had left it so long before calling him.

I could hear my husband praying with all his heart. He just prayed and prayed. I heard them say that the baby was in shock and was not making any noise; my husband was shouting and asking them what was going on and what they meant when they said that the baby was not responding. I tried to ask what was happening but my tongue seemed to have become very large. I looked at my hands which were now completely black and had become very large. I said, "Lord, I need to get home to look after my children, don't let me die, help me". I became very weak. I remember seeing a nurse covered in blood and I thought that she had been covered in my blood. I could hear my husband speaking in tongues; he did not care that everyone was looking at him; I could hear hysteria in his voice.

Suddenly, it was all over. They stitched me and sent me to the Recovery Room. I passed out. The next day I was told that the whole Delivery Ward was shut down that day because a woman's Caesarean operation had gone wrong and she was in a critical condition, and they did not know if she or the baby would survive. To Jesus be all the glory, I survived and so did the baby.

I praise and thank the Lord Jesus Christ for his great

190

mercies toward me; I thank him again and again for the power of prayer. What would I have done without the prayers my husband prayed. He prayed; he prayed; he prayed with all his heart. In my weakness, I asked my dear Lord to spare my life and he did, and the baby's. Today my baby is a lovely boy who has intellectual ability. Thank God for Jesus.

A point of note: Since my operation, the Maternity Ward at that hospital has closed down because of the record number of deaths by Caesarean section there.

From experience I would advise anyone going into any hospital to undergo any form of operation, however simple it may seem, please ensure that you go there with someone who knows how to pray. Prayer brought me out and it will bring you out of every difficult situation. The best person to stand with you in every condition of life is our blessed and compassionate Lord Jesus Christ. Ask the Lord to send angels to accompany you, because man makes mistakes which only God can correct. *Luke 1:37 For with God nothing shall be impossible.*

I do hope my testimony helps someone.

Blessings.

MY TESTIMONY
JESUS KEPT MY SON ALIVE
By Sister A-K

O give thanks unto the Lord; for he is good: for his mercy endureth for ever. [Psalm 136:1].

On 9th April 2009 I was on my way to Peckham, preparing myself for Easter. I received a phone call from my older son to say that Mike was knocked off his bike. I did not know what to do, being so far away in Peckham; the accident took place in Kennington. I panicked and ran all the way from Peckham to Camberwell. It seems that on the day when one thing goes wrong every thing seems to go wrong. I had no minutes on my phone to make a call; there was no car at the cab office, no bus going in my direction; my friend's car had no petrol. The police kept phoning me; also my older son, and all who had heard about the accident.

Jesus is wonderful. Help came for me. My friend stopped one of the mother's who had come to collect her child from school and asked her to take me to where the accident had taken place. However, when I got there my son had already been air-lifted to White Chapel Hospital. The police then took me and my older son by their car to the hospital. On arriving at the hospital, the sight of my son was more than I could bear: He was three times his normal size; his head was covered in blood; his eyes were wide open; both sides were cut open with tubes coming out. The doctor looking after him tried to explain to me what was taking place but said my son was doing nothing; was on a life support machine; and his heart had started to crumble. I did not know what to do so I went outside and just walked up and down. I said, "Lord, this is too

192

much for me to bear; I leave it all in your hands". After a couple of hours they transferred him to Great Ormond Street Hospital [a specialist Children's Hospital] because his condition was severe. At this hospital they placed him in Intensive Care on a life support machine for a week. The doctor told me his condition was critical and it could get worse. Here is the medical diagnosis: Lungs collapsed; Liver bruised; Face fractured; Internal bleeding; Head burst in three places; brain injured. The doctor booked me a room at the hospital so I could get some rest. My rest was prayer. I had to pray. I needed the help of the Lord as never before. I went on my knees before the Lord with tears flowing and asked the Lord to forgive any sin my son had committed. I said, "Lord if he has been rude, please don't take his life as punishment; give him another chance. Lord, I promise to give you my life as a living sacrifice; I will worship you. Please cover us with your blood of protection". I wept before the Lord.

After a week, my son started to breathe on his own, but he couldn't do any of the following: see, walk, talk, sit, move, remember anything. He had to have therapy to enable him to do any of these, but the grace of the Lord Jesus Christ kept me, although I was not able to eat or sleep properly. I prayed and believed the Lord to see me through and he gave me the strength to cope. Jesus Christ is Lord. Prayer really works.

My son, Mike, recovered so quickly the doctors were astonished. They feared that his body might get into shock because he was healing too quickly, but they did not understand that I prayed to a miracle working God who was in control of my son's recovery. Mike remained in hospital for over six months and was on therapy treatment for over two years.

193

As Mike recovered, I noticed a difference in my own life. I was drawn to the Lord in a deeper commitment and gave up my old ways of sinful living; I developed a hunger for the word of God and I thirsted for more of God. One day I went to Brixton where I met a friend and began telling her about the love of the Lord; as I did this I began to cry and I heard myself say, "Be careful what you promise the Lord". I there and then remembered that I had promised the Lord that I would give my life sacrificially to him if he spared the life of my son.

I have surrendered my life completely to the Lord. I am saved and baptized and I love the Lord with my whole heart. Thank God for Jesus; thank God for prayer; thank God for his mercies toward me; thank God for sparing the life of my son; thank God for loving me and for saving me from sin and satan, from the world, the flesh and the devil.

My desire is that many souls will find Jesus as their personal saviour as I have, and get their deliverance. If you do not know Jesus as your Lord, you can receive him right now. No one knows what will happen along life's journey and from my own experience, Jesus can take you out of the worst situation. Mine was really bad but with prayer the Lord brought me out. He will do the same for you if you turn to him. If you never prayed before, begin to pray because prayer is powerful and Jesus hears and answers prayers.

I hope my testimony helps someone and gives someone hope where the condition seems impossible, because there is hope in God.

God bless you.

APPENDIX 2

JESUS SAVES

Jesus is coming again for a prepared people to take them to a place he has prepared for them. *[St John 14:2-3]*. In this life we must overcome the troubles and trials caused by sin and satan. We cannot overcome in our own strength, we need the Lord to enable us to do this. So you may ask: How do I prepare myself for that prepared place, and how do I overcome to get there? Answer: You must be born again; you must be saved. Question: How do I get born again; how do I get saved? Here is the bible way to go about it.

*Matthew 1:21 And she shall bring forth a son, and thou shalt call his name **JESUS**: for he shall save his people from their sins.*

Jesus died for you; he paid the price for your sins and a few simple words in line with the scriptures will put you into heaven at this very moment. Just follow these simple steps below and you are assured of victory, in the name of Jesus:

1] *Repent:* Lord, I repent of all my sins. I am sorry to have displeased you for such a long time. Please forgive me. I now forgive all who have wronged me, in the name of Jesus.

2] *Confess:* Holy Father, I confess that Jesus died for my sins according to the scriptures; that he rose from the dead for my justification; that he ascended into heaven and ever lives to make intercession for me.

3]   *Request Salvation:* Lord, please save me from all my sins and help me to live a victorious Christian life, in the name of the Lord Jesus Christ.

4]   *Thanksgiving:* Thank you Lord for saving me. Thank you Jesus. I am now a child of God, praise the Lord.

You are now saved, and as you read the bible and pray, the Lord will open your understanding to spiritual things.

5]   Find a bible believing church to attend and receive fellowship: Ask the Lord to show you a church where the truth is being taught so that you may have fellowship with other believers.

6]   Tell your family, relatives and friends about your new found faith. Tell them how wonderful you feel about having Jesus as your personal saviour.

Ephesians 6:10   Finally, my brethren, be strong in the Lord and in the power of his might.

1 Corinthians 1:9   God is faithful, by whom ye were called unto the fellowship of his Son Jesus Christ our Lord.

APPENDIX 3

SOME SCRIPTURE VERSES YOU SHOULD KNOW/MEMORISE

Here are a few scripture verses we should all memorise for our edification and comfort:

Amos 4:12 Therefore thus will I do unto thee, O Israel: and because I will do this unto thee, prepare to meet thy God, O Israel.

Matthew 25:6, 35-36 6. And at midnight there was a cry made, Behold, the bridegroom cometh; go ye out to meet him. 35. For I was an hungred, and ye gave me meat: I was thirsty, and ye gave me drink: I was a stranger, and ye took me in: 36. Naked and ye clothed me: I was sick, and ye visited me: I was in prison, and ye came unto me.

Matthew 25:34 Then shall the King say unto them on his right hand, Come ye blessed of my Father, inherit the kingdom prepared for you from the foundation of the world.

1 Thessalonians 4:16-17 16. For the Lord himself shall descend from heaven with a shout, with the voice of the archangel, and with the trump of God: and the dead in Christ shall rise first. 17. Then we which are alive and remain shall be caught up together with them in the clouds, to meet the Lord in the air: and so shall we ever be with the Lord.

1 Corinthians 2:9 But as it is written, Eye hath not seen, nor ear heard, neither have entered in the heart of man, the things which God hath prepared for them that love him.

1 Corinthians 15: 50-52, 57 50. *Now this I say, brethren, that flesh and blood cannot inherit the kingdom of God; neither doth corruption inherit incorruption. 51. Behold, I shew you a mystery; We shall not all sleep, but we shall all be changed. 52. In a moment, in the twinkling of an eye, at the last trump: for the trumpet shall sound, and the dead shall be raised incorruptible, and we shall be changed. 57. But thanks be to God, which giveth us the victory through our Lord Jesus Christ.*

Mark 13:33, 37 *Take ye heed, watch and pray: for ye know not when the time is. 37. And what I say unto you I say unto all, Watch.*

Matthew 24:35 *Heaven and earth shall pass away, but my words shall not pass away.*

Revelation 21:3-4,8 3. *And I heard a great voice out of heaven saying, Behold the tabernacle of God is with men, and he will dwell with them, and they shall be his people, and God himself shall be with them, and be their God. 4. And God shall wipe away all tears from their eyes; and there shall be no more death, neither sorrow, nor crying, neither shall there be any more pain: for the former things are passed away. 8. But the fearful, and unbelieving, and the abominable, and murderers, and whoremongers, and sorcerers, and idolaters, and all liars shall have their part in the lake which burneth with fire and brimstone, which is the second death.*

Revelation 22:12 *And behold, I come quickly, and my reward is with me, to give every man according as his work shall be.*

198

Revelation 20:12-14 *12. And I saw the dead, small and great, stand before God; and the books were opened: and another book was opened, which is the book of life: and the dead were judged out of those things which were written in the books, according to their works. 13. And the sea gave up the dead which were in it, and death and hell delivered up the dead which were in them; and they were judged every man according to their works. 14. And death and hell were cast into the lake of fire. This is the second death.*

Revelation 20:10 *And the devil that deceived them was cast into the lake of fire and brimstone, where the beast and the false prophet are, and shall be tormented day and night for ever and ever.*

Revelation 19: 14, 16 *14. And the armies which were in heaven followed him upon white horses, clothed in fine linen, white and clean. 16. And he hath on his vesture and on his thigh a name written,* **KING OF KINGS, AND LORD OF LORDS.**

Ecclesiastes 12:13-14 *Let us hear the conclusion of the whole matter: fear God and keep his commandments: for this is the whole duty of man. For God shall bring every work into judgment, with every secret thing, whether it be good, or whether it be evil.*

Mark 13:37 *And what I say unto you I say unto all,* **Watch.**

Praise the Lord.

OTHER BOOKS BY THE AUTHOR

Christ's Hand on my Life [2004]
Why I Despise Witchcraft [2005]
The Blood of Jesus Revealed [2005]
The Wonderful Name of Jesus [2005]
You are an Angel [2007]
Powerful Testimonies and the Word of God [2008]
Who is Jesus Christ (1) [2009]
Who is Jesus Christ (2) [2009]
Our Father which art in Heaven [2009]
PRAYER – Men Ought Always to Pray [2010]
The Blood of Jesus Christ and the Resurrection [2011]

ALSO MANY BOOKLETS INCLUDING:

The Godhead
Tithes and Offerings
Tithing and the Seventh Day Sabbath
Your Silver and your Gold
The Wonder of the Atonement

To contact the Author write to:

Apostolic Church of God 7th Day Ministries
P O Box 304
Harrow Middlesex
HA2 0YQ
United Kingdom

Website: www.acog7.org.uk
E-mail: lake22d@aol.com